MORE KnitWits

MORE KnitWits

20 More Fun Projects for Those Who Love to Knit & Purl

KATIE BOYETTE

SELLERS
PUBLISHING

Published by **Sellers Publishing, Inc.**
161 John Roberts Road, South Portland, Maine 04106

Visit our Web Site: www.sellerspublishing.com
E-mail: rsp@rsvp.com

Design and layout copyright © BlueRed Press Ltd 2011
Text copyright © Katie Boyette
Patterns and templates copyright © Katie Boyette
All rights reserved.
Design by Matt Windsor

ISBN 13: 978-1-4162-0644-6
Library of Congress Number 2011922416

10 9 8 7 6 5 4 3 2 1

Printed and Bound in China

Knitting Needle Sizes

Metric (mm)	U.S.
2.0	0
2.25	1
2.75	2
3.0	-
3.25	3
3.5	4
3.75	5
4.0	6
4.5	7
5.0	8
5.5	9
6.0	10
6.5	10.5
7.0	-
7.5	-
8.0	11
9.0	13
10.0	15
12.75	17
15.0	19
19.0	35
25.0	50

courtesy of the Craft Yarn Council, Gastonia, N.C.

Contents

Introduction

My hometown is a small and friendly mountain college town. It doesn't take long to become familiar with the locals. If my hometown folks were to describe me, they would probably say, "that girl who knits all the time". It's an accurate description. I do knit all the time. One of my very favorite things about knitting toys is their portability. I knit in the coffee shop, at the bar, at restaurants while waiting on my food, in line at the bank, on the bleachers at my son's soccer games, at work when my boss isn't looking, and even in my car while waiting at a long stoplight. I'm a fidgety person, and knitting keeps my hands busy.

Admittedly, the other thing I love about knitting my odd toys are the quizzical looks I get when people ask me what I'm working on. "What are you knitting?" asked another soccer mom at practice recently, to which I responded, "Well . . . it's a toilet . . . a toilet who's eating someone." I'm certain she expected me to say "mittens" or "a hat." She paused and then responded with a confused laugh. I enjoy these reactions. I love showing people how versatile and interesting knitting can be. I love teddy bears and bunnies as much as the next kid, but there is so much more you can do with yarn.

When I was learning to knit, I had an intense hunger for cute and funny toy patterns. In the spirit of keeping an open mind while designing potential projects, I like to take toy inspiration from all sorts of things. Sometimes I have my daughter draw a picture, or describe a bad dream she's had. I love the way my daughter can animate anything in the house. She'll pick up her fork, give it a deep voice, and the next thing you know, it's marrying the butter knife. Sometimes I look around the house, and imagine one of the appliances or fixtures attacking me, hence the scary toilet. I like to tell myself, that given some careful measurements and the right gauge swatch, I can recreate anything in knitted form. Of course, take one look at the shelf full of abandoned knitting projects, and you'll know this isn't true at all, but I try to limit myself as little as possible.

So I hope you'll enjoy knitting these new projects as much as I've enjoyed creating them. I hope you'll also elicit a few laughs and smiles from the people you make them for.

Katie Boyette

Flash

Like so many monsters in their mid-forties, Flash began having problems with his eyesight. It started when he was having trouble reading his favorite romance novels. Then he started making mathematical errors when balancing his checkbook. But he was stubborn, and didn't want to confront his age, so his eyesight grew worse and worse. One day he leaned in to kiss his wife, only to realize he was smooching the mailman, who was not amused, so he relented and paid a visit to the eye doctor. He was told he needed bifocals, and, of course, they had to be custom made for the monster with five eyes. They were not cheap, but the mailman thinks they're worth every penny.

Materials

- 1 skein Cascade 220 in 9561 (MC)
- 1 skein Cascade 220 in 4147 (CC)
- 1 set US size 6 (4.00mm) double pointed needles
- 1 pair US size 6 (4.00mm) straight needles
- Yarn needle
- Embroidery needle
- Craft felt in black and white
- Embroidery floss in black and white
- Toy stuffing

Gauge:
20 sts and 26 rows over 4 in. in stockinette st

Finished toy size:
8 in. tall.

Glossary of abbreviations

CO	cast on
k	knit
k2tog	knit two together
kfb	knit into front and back of stitch
pm	place marker
ssk	slip, slip, knit slipped stitches together
st[s]	stitch[es]

Body, knit from the top down
Using MC, CO6, pm, join to knit in the round.
Round 1: Kfb 6 times. 12 sts
Round 2 and all even numbered rounds: Knit.
Round 3: (Kfb, k1) 6 times. 18 sts
Round 5: (K4, kfb, k3, kfb) twice. 22 sts
Round 7: (K4, kfb, k5, kfb) twice. 26 sts
Round 9: (Kfb, k2, kfb twice, k7, kfb) twice. 34 sts
Round 11: (K6, kfb, k9, kfb) twice. 38 sts
Round 13: (K6, kfb, k11, kfb) twice. 42 sts
Round 15: (Kfb, k4, kfb twice, k13, kfb) twice. 50 sts
Round 17: (K8, kfb, k15, kfb) twice. 54 sts
Round 19: (K8, kfb, k17, kfb) twice. 58 sts
Round 21: (Kfb, k6, kfb twice, k19, kfb) twice. 66 sts
Rounds 22–44: Knit.

Begin diving for legs
Place the first 16 sts on a piece of scrap yarn. Place the next 11 sts on a double pointed needle. Place the next 22 sts on another piece of scrap yarn for second leg. Place the next 11 sts on one double pointed needle. Place the remaining 6 sts on the first piece of scrap yarn with the first 16 sts. This will be the first leg. Reconnect MC to knit the sts on one of the double pointed needles. Knit 10 rows in stockinette st, (see figure 1). Break yarn, leaving a 12 in. tail. Use the tail and a kitchener stitch to graft the sts from the double pointed needles together. This is the crotch. Stuff the body firmly.

Legs
Reconnect MC to begin the first leg. Pick up and knit the 22 sts from one of the pieces of scrap yarn, diving sts between double pointed needles. Pick up and knit 10 sts from the inside edge of the crotch. Pm, join to knit in the round. 32 sts, (see figure 2).
Knit 6 rounds even.
Round 7: (K2tog, k6, ssk, k6) twice. 28 sts
Round 8: (K2tog, k1, ssk, k6) twice. 24 sts

Round 9: (K2tog, k2) 6 times. 18 sts
Round 10: (K2tog, k1) 6 times. 12 sts
Round 11: K2tog 6 times. 6 sts
Break yarn, pull tail through remaining sts, knot pull tail to inside of foot. Stuff foot. Reconnect MC and knit second foot same as for first, pausing to stuff second foot before closing it up.

Arms (knit 2)
Using MC, CO6, pm, join to knit in the round.
Round 1: (K1, kfb, k1) twice. 8 sts
Round 2: (K1, kfb twice, k1) twice. 12 sts
Round 3: (K1, kfb, k2, kfb, k1) twice. 16 sts
Round 4: (K1, kfb, k4, kfb, k1) twice. 20 sts
Round 5: (K1, kfb, k6, kfb, k1) twice. 24 sts
Rounds 6–9: Knit.
Round 10: (K1, k2tog, k6, ssk, k1) twice. 20 sts
Round 11: Knit.

Round 12: K1, k2tog, k14, ssk, k1. 18 sts
Round 13: Knit.
Round 14: K1, k2tog, k12, ssk, k1. 16 sts
Round 15: Knit.
Round 16: K1, k2tog, k10, ssk, k1. 14 sts
Round 17: Knit.
Round 18: K1, k2tog, k8, ssk, k1. 12 sts
Bind off. Stuff arm lightly.

Belly
Using straight needles and CC, CO13.
Row 1: K1, kfb, k9, kfb, k1. 15 sts

Row 2 and all even rows: Purl.
Row 3: K1, kfb, k11, kfb, k1. 17 sts
Row 5: K1, kfb, k13, kfb, k1. 19 sts
Rows 6–8: Complete in stockinette st
Row 9: K1, k2tog, k13, ssk, k1. 17 sts
Row 11: K1, k2tog, k11, ssk, k1. 15 sts
Row 13: K1, k2tog, k9, ssk, k1. 13 sts
Bind off purlwise.

Long hair (knit 2)
Using CC and two double pointed needles, CO1. Knit as an i-cord,

increasing as follows:
Row 1: Kfb. 2 sts
Row 2: Kfb, k1. 3 sts
Knit 4 more rows. Bind off.

Short hair (knit 3)
Using CC and double pointed needles, CO1. Knit as an i-cord, increasing as follows:
Row 1: Kfb. 2 sts
Knit 3 more rows. Bind off.

Assembly

Seam the arms to the sides of body, (see figure 3).
Seam the belly to the front of the body using CC and running stitch, (see figure 4).
Seam the hair to the top of the head.
Curl into shape with fingers, (see figure 5).
Cut felt pieces using the template. Sew the eyes to the face using corresponding thread color, (see figure 6).
Use a piece of black embroidery floss to create mouth.

1

Upper Right Eyeball
and Pupil

Upper Left Eyeball
and Pupil

Lower Right Eyeball
and Pupil

Centre Eyeball
and Pupil

Lower Left Eyeball
and Pupil

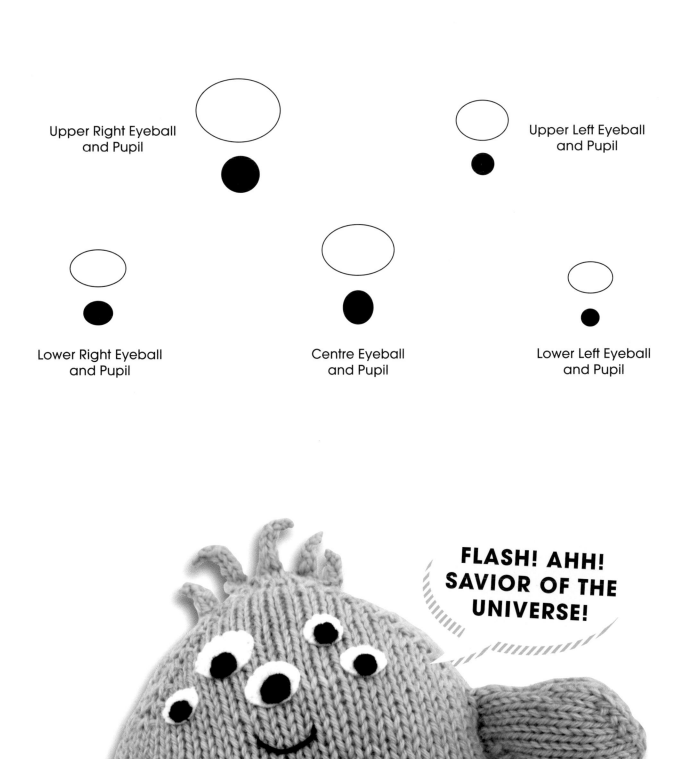

**FLASH! AHH!
SAVIOR OF THE
UNIVERSE!**

Doodle

Like most roosters, Doodle just loves to dance. But you won't find Doodle at the club. No, Doodle is a serious, competitive ballroom dancer. It's good thing he's so talented; he certainly can't rely on his surly disposition to win him a dance partner. Growing up in Argentina, he came to prefer the Tango, but you may occasionally find him dancing the Lindy Hop or Salsa. To pay for his expensive collection of performance tuxedos, he also teaches Zumba classes at the local gym.

Materials

- 1 skein Cascade 220 in 8414 (MC)
- 1 skein Cascade 220 in 2436 (CC)
- 1 set US size 6 (4.00mm) double pointed needles
- 1 pair US size 6 (4.00mm) straight needles
- Pieces of wool felt in white, black, orange, and dark red
- Toy stuffing
- Yarn needle
- Embroidery needle
- Embroidery floss in white, black, orange, and dark red

Gauge:
20 sts and 26 rows over 4 in. in stockinette st

Finished toy size:
11 in. tall.

Glossary of abbreviations

CO	cast on
k	knit
k2tog	knit two together
kfb	knit into front and back of stitch
p	purl
pm	place marker
ssk	slip, slip, knit slipped stitches together
st[s]	stitch[es]
St st	stockinette stitch

Body, knit from the top down
Using US size 6 (4.00mm) double pointed needles and MC, CO28, pm, join to knit in the round.
Round 1: (K1, kfb, k10, kfb, k1) twice. 32 sts
Round 2: Knit.
Round 3: (K1, kfb, k12, kfb, k1) twice. 36 sts
Round 4: K1, kfb, k32, kfb, k1. 38 sts
Round 5: (K1, kfb, k15, kfb, k1) twice. 42 sts
Round 6: K1, kfb, k38, kfb, k1. 44 sts
Round 7: (K1, kfb, k18, kfb, k1) twice. 48 sts
Round 8: K1, kfb, k44, kfb, k1. 50 sts
Round 9: K1, kfb, k46, kfb, k1. 52 sts
Round 10: K1, kfb, k48, kfb, k1. 54 sts
Round 11: K1, kfb, k50, kfb, k1. 56 sts
Round 12: Knit.
Round 13: K1, kfb, k52, kfb, k1. 58 sts
Round 14: Knit.
Round 15: K1, kfb, k54, kfb, k1. 60 sts
Round 16: Knit.

Round 17: K1, kfb, k56, kfb, k1. 62 sts
Round 18–32: Knit.
Round 33: (K1, k2tog, k27, ssk, k1) twice. 58 sts
Rounds 34–39: Knit.
Round 40: (K1, kfb, k25, ssk, k1) twice. 54 sts
Rounds 41–46: Knit.
Break yarn. Place sts on a piece of scrap yarn.

Tail
Using US size 6 (4.00mm) double pointed needles and MC, CO4, pm, join to knit in the round.
Round 1: Kfb, k2, kfb. 6 sts
Round 2: Knit.
Round 3: Kfb, k4, kfb. 8 sts
Round 4: Knit.
Round 5: (K1, kfb twice, k1) twice. 12 sts
Round 6: Knit.
Round 7: K4, kfb, k2, kfb, k4. 14 sts
Round 8: K5, kfb, k2, kfb, k5. 16 sts
Round 9: K6, kfb, k2, kfb, k6. 18 sts

Round 10: K7, kfb, k2, kfb, k7. 20 sts
Round 11: K8, kfb, k2, kfb, k8. 22 sts
Divide sts for tail evenly between 2 double pointed needles.
Join tail to body as follows: Rejoin yarn to body where it was cut. Using one needle, pick up and knit across the first 27 sts. On the same needle, knit across the first 11 sts from tail. Using a second needle, pick up and knit across the remaining 11 sts from tail. On the same needle, knit across the remaining 27 sts from body. Pm, continue to knit the body in the round, (see figure 1). 76 sts
Round 1: (K1, k2tog, k32, ssk, k1) twice. 72 sts
Round 2: Knit.
Round 3: (K1, k2tog, k30, ssk, k1) twice. 68 sts
Round 4: Knit.
Round 5: (K1, k2tog, k28, ssk, k1) twice. 64 sts
Round 6: Knit.
Round 7: (K1, k2tog, k26, ssk, k1) twice.

60 sts
Round 8: Knit.
Round 9: (K1, k2tog, k24, ssk, k1) twice.
56 sts
Round 10: Knit.
Round 11: (K1, k2tog, k22, ssk, k1)
twice. 52 sts
Round 12: Knit.
Round 13: (K1, k2tog, k20, ssk, k1)
twice. 48 sts
Round 14: Knit.
Round 15: (K1, k2tog, k18, ssk, k1)
twice. 44 sts
Round 16: Knit.
Round 17: (K1, k2tog, k16, ssk, k1)
twice. 40 sts
Round 18: Knit.
Round 19: (K1, k2tog, k14, ssk, k1)
twice. 36 sts
Round 20: Knit.
Round 21: (K1, k2tog, k12, ssk, k1)

twice. 32 sts
Round 22: Knit.
Round 23: (K1, k2tog, k10, ssk, k1)
twice. 28 sts
Round 24: Knit.
Round 25: (K1, k2tog, k8, ssk, k1) twice.
24 sts
Bind off, leaving an 18 in. tail for seaming.

Chest
Using US size 6 (4.00mm) straight
needles and CC, CO6.
Row 1: K1, kfb, k2, kfb, k1. 8 sts
Row 2 and all even rows: Purl.
Row 3: K1, kfb, k4, kfb, k1. 10 sts
Row 5: K1, kfb, k6, kfb, k1. 12 sts
Row 7: K1, kfb, k8, kfb, k1. 14 sts
Row 9: K1, kfb, k10, kfb, k1. 16 sts
Row 11: K1, kfb, k12, kfb, k1. 18 sts
Row 13: K1, kfb, k14, kfb, k1. 20 sts
Rows 14–18: Complete in stockinette st.

Row 19: K1, k2tog, k14, ssk, k1. 18 sts
Row 21: K1, k2tog, k12, ssk, k1. 16 sts
Row 23: K1, k2tog, k10, ssk, k1. 14 sts
Row 25: K1, k2tog, k8, ssk, k1. 12 sts
Row 27: K1, k2tog, k6, ssk, k1. 10 sts
Row 29: K1, k2tog, k4, ssk, k1. 8 sts
Row 31: K1, k2tog, k2, ssk, k1. 6 sts
Bind off purlwise.

Feet (make 2)
For middle toe:
Using CC and US size 6 (4.00mm)
double pointed needles, CO4. Knit a
1 in. piece of i-cord.
For two outside toes:
Using CC and double pointed needles,
CO4. Knit a ½ in. piece of i-cord.
Place small toes along each side of middle
toe, halfway down, and seam into place.

Assembly

Use a yarn needle to seam up the top of
the head. Stuff the body firmly, pressing
flat as you go to get the bird's shape.
Seam the bottom of the body,
(see figure 2).
Center the chest over the body. Pin into
place. Use a piece of CC and a running
stitch to hold into place. Pause when ¾
of the way done to lightly stuff chest,
(see figure 3).
Cut felt pieces using template. Using red
thread, sew together the two pieces of
the crest.
Center the crest on the head and sew
into place, (see figure 4).
Fold the beak in half and center on side
of the face. Sew into place using orange
thread, (see figure 5).
Sew the eyes onto each side of the
head, using a corresponding color of
thread, (see figure 6).
Place the feet on the underside of the
body. Use the tail to seam into place,
(see figure 7).

1

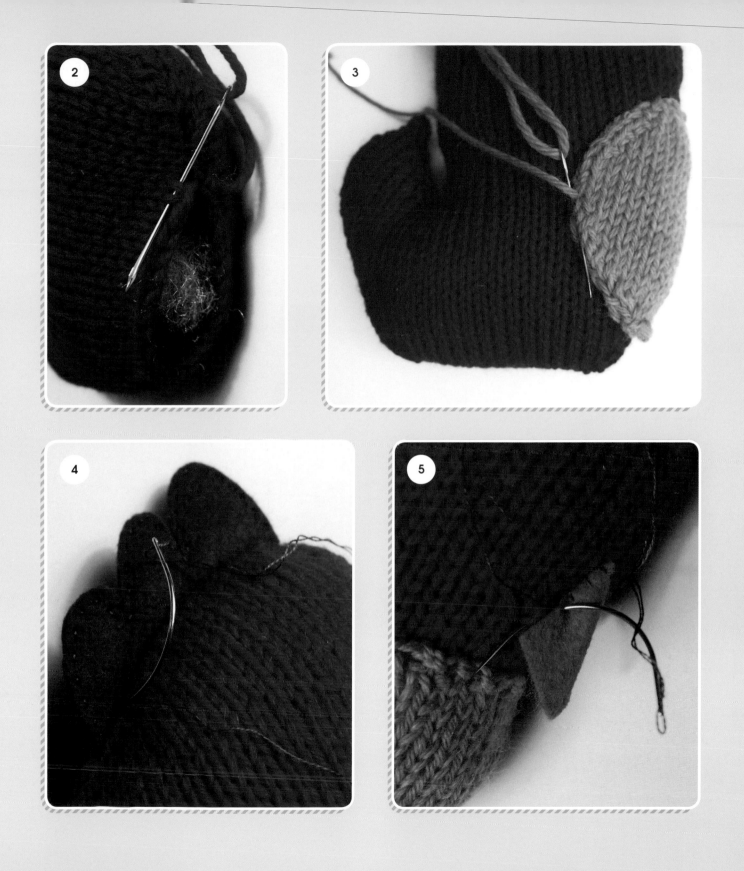

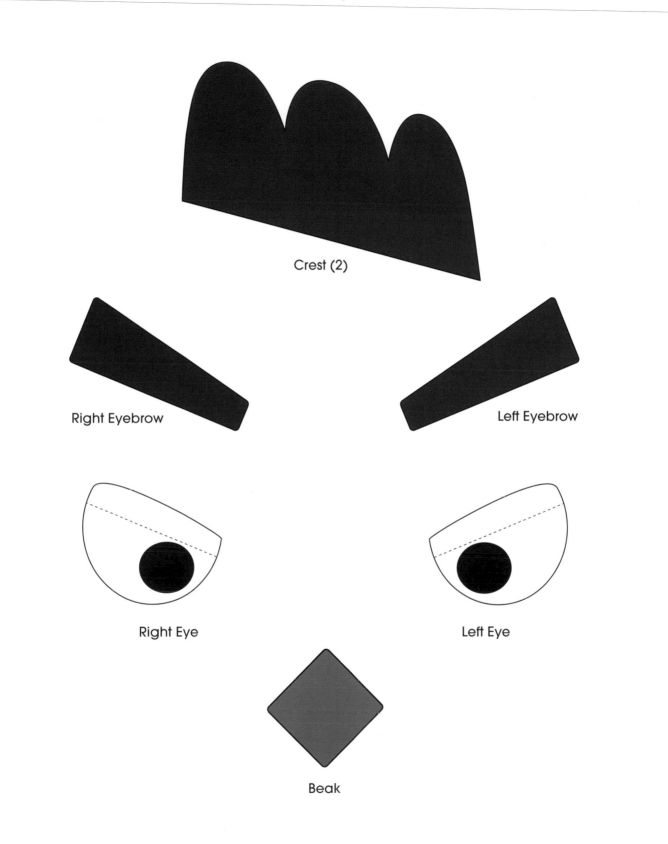

Crest (2)

Right Eyebrow

Left Eyebrow

Right Eye

Left Eye

Beak

Turnip

Turnip thinks he's a peacock. You and I both know he's not, of course. The plumage on his head is pretty, but not nearly as showy and magnificent as a peacock. And then there is the fact that he only has one eye. But you couldn't convince Turnip that he's any less fantastic. Even a passing glance will cause him to puff out his chest, unfold the small feathers atop his head, and strut about like royalty.

Materials

- 1 skein Cascade 220 in 9455
- Scrap of black yarn
- 1 set US size 6 (4.00mm) double pointed needles
- 1 pair US size 6 (4.00mm) straight needles
- Yarn needle
- Embroidery needle
- Craft felt in black, white, blue, and orange
- Embroidery floss in black, white, and orange
- Toy stuffing

Gauge:
20 sts and 26 rows over 4 in. in stockinette st

Finished toy size:
9½ in. tall.

Glossary of abbreviations

CO	cast on
k	knit
k2tog	knit two together
kfb	knit into front and back of stitch
p	purl
pm	place marker
ssk	slip, slip, knit slipped stitches together
st[s]	stitch[es]

Body, knit from the top down
Using MC, CO6, pm, join to knit in the round.
Round 1: Kfb 6 times. 12 sts
Round 2 and all even numbered rounds: Knit.
Round 3: (Kfb, k1) 6 times. 18 sts
Round 5: (Kfb, k2) 6 times. 24 sts
Round 7: (Kfb, k3) 6 times. 30 sts
Round 9: (Kfb, k4) 6 times. 36 sts
Round 11: (Kfb, k5) 6 times. 42 sts
Round 13: (Kfb, k6) 6 times. 48 sts
Round 15: (Kfb, k7) 6 times. 54 sts
Round 17: (Kfb, k8) 6 times. 60 sts
Round 19: (Kfb, k9) 6 times. 66 sts
Round 21: (Kfb, k10) 6 times. 72 sts
Rounds 22–36: Knit.
Round 37: (K2tog, k10) 6 times. 66 sts
Round 39: (K2tog, k9) 6 times. 60 sts
Round 41: (K2tog, k8) 6 times. 54 sts
Round 43: (K2tog, k7) 6 times. 48 sts
Begin dividing for legs
Knit the first 24 sts, dividing them between 3 needles as you go, 8 sts on each needle. Place the last 24 sts on a piece of scrap yarn. Using a 4th needle, CO8 sts as the inside edge of the first leg. Pm, join to knit in the round, (see figure 1). Stuff the body before beginning knitting.
Rounds 1: Knit. 32 sts
Round 2: K2tog, k20, ssk, k8. 30 sts
Round 3: Knit.
Round 4: K2tog, k8, k2tog, k8, ssk, k8. 27 sts
Round 5: Knit.
Round 6: K2tog, k7, k2tog, k6, ssk, k8. 24 sts
Round 7: Knit.
Round 8: (K2tog, k3) 6 times. 18 sts
Round 9: Knit.
Round 10: (K2tog, k2) 6 times. 12 sts
Round 11: K2tog 6 times. 6 sts
Break yarn, pull tail through remaining sts, knot, pull tail to inside of toy.
Stuff knitted leg. Reattach yarn between legs. Knit the 24 sts from the scrap yarn, dividing between 3 needles, 8 sts per needle. With a 4th needle, pick up and knit 8 sts from the inside edge of the first leg. Pm, join to knit in the round. Follow the same directions as for first leg, pausing near the end to stuff leg before closing up sts.

Wings (knit 2)
Using MC, and straight needles, CO14.
Row 1: Knit.
Row 2: K1, k2tog, k8, ssk, k1. 12 sts
Row 3: Knit.
Row 4: K1, k2tog, k6, ssk, k1. 10 sts
Row 5: Knit.
Row 6: K1, k2tog, k4, ssk, k1. 8 sts
Row 7: Knit.
Row 8: K1, k2tog, k2, ssk, k1. 6 sts
Row 9: Knit.
Row 10: K1, k2tog, ssk, k1. 4 sts
Break yarn, draw tail through remaining sts. Weave tail into purl side of wing.

Large feathers (knit 2)
Using MC, and straight needles, CO1 st.
Row 1: Kfb. 2 sts
Row 2: Kfb twice. 4 sts
Row 3: K1, kfb twice, k1. 6 sts
Row 4–5: Knit.
Row 6: K1, k2tog, ssk, k1. 4 sts
Row 7: K2tog, ssk. 2 sts
Switch to black yarn. Knit remaining 2 sts as an i-cord for 3 rows. Bind off, leaving a 4 in. tail for seaming.

Small feather

Using MC, and straight needles, CO1 st.
Row 1: Kfb. 2 sts
Row 2: Kfb twice. 4 sts
Rows 3–4: Knit.
Row 5: K2tog, ssk. 2 sts
Switch to black yarn. Knit remaining
2 sts as an i-cord for 3 rows. Bind off,
leaving a 4 in. tail for seaming.

Assembly

Seam the wings to the sides of the body, knit side out.

Cut felt pieces from the template. Use the corresponding color of embroidery floss to attach the eye to the head, beginning with the white center, following with the black upper edge, (see figure 2). Sew on the pupil and the iris. The bottom of the eye is created with an outline stitch. Use a small length of black yarn to create bottom line under eye, securing in place with a single strand of embroidery floss, (see figure 3). Use white floss to create a reflection in the eye, (see figure 4).

Sew the feathers to the top of the head, using tail of yarn, (see figure 5).

Sew the beak to the face, using orange floss, (see figure 6).

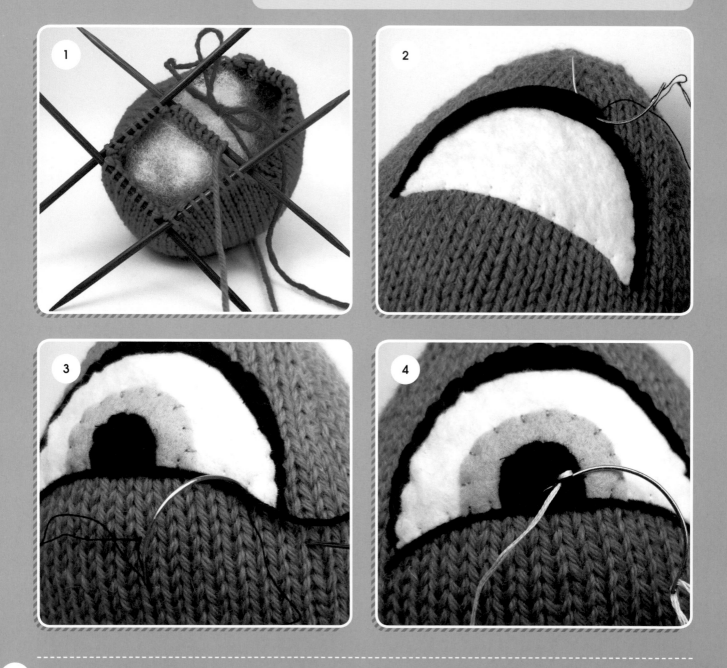

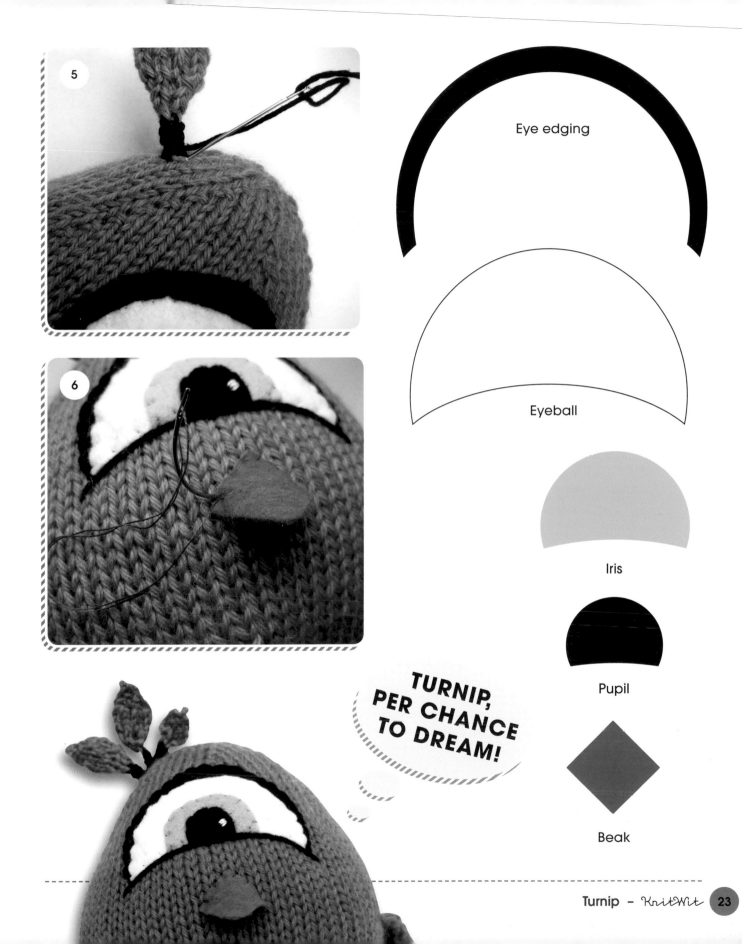

5

6

Eye edging

Eyeball

Iris

Pupil

TURNIP, PER CHANCE TO DREAM!

Beak

Tony

Tony is a loud talker. Tony is so loud the neighbors can hear every conversation he has, even several blocks away. They know that he lied last Thursday when he called in sick to work, because they saw him the very same morning jumping on the trampoline in his backyard. They know that he calls his mom every night to hear a bedtime story. They know that his secret pet name for his girlfriend is "butter bean." It's not that the neighbors are nosy. They despise the excessive noise. Tony has spent a fortune on noise violation fines. He just can't help his very powerful vocal chords. It isn't all bad though. Tony got a job as the announcer at the local ball field. He doesn't even need a microphone.

Materials

- 1 skein Cascade 220 in 2404 (MC)
- 1 skein Cascade 220 in 8339 (CC)
- 1 set US size 6 (4.00mm) double pointed needles
- Yarn needle
- Embroidery needle
- Craft felt in black, white, and red
- Embroidery floss in black, white, and red
- Toy stuffing

Gauge:
20 sts and 26 rows over 4 in. in stockinette st

Finished toy size:
8 in. tall.

Glossary of abbreviations

CO	cast on
k	knit
k2tog	knit two together
Kfb	knit into front and back of stitch
pm	place marker
ssk	slip, slip, knit slipped stitches together
st[s]	stitch[es]

A note about knitting stripes in the round

When knitting stripes in the round, there will be a step where the colors change. To prevent this, you may choose to use a jogless join:

On color change rounds, change colors by knitting the first stitch of the new color as you usually would. Then, knit the rest of the stitches to the end of the round. On the next round, slip the first stitch of the new color, then knit the rest of the stitches. On every following round, knit every stitch as usual.

Body, knit from the head down

Using MC, CO6, pm, join to knit in the round.

Round 1: Kfb 6 times. 12 sts
Round 2 and all even numbered rounds: Knit.
Round 3: (Kfb, k1) 6 times. 18 sts
Round 5: (Kfb, k2) 6 times. 24 sts
Round 6: Knit. Change to CC. Run MC along the back, twisting sts as you go.

Continue to switch colors every 6 rounds, (see figure 1).
Round 7: (Kfb, k3) 6 times. 30 sts
Round 9: (Kfb, k4) 6 times. 36 sts
Round 11: (Kfb, k5) 6 times. 42 sts
Round 13: (Kfb, k6) 6 times. 48 sts
Round 15: (Kfb, k7) 6 times. 54 sts
Round 17: (Kfb, k8) 6 times. 60 sts
Rounds 18–42: Knit, ending with the last round of a MC stripe. Break yarn.

Begin dividing for legs

Using CC, knit the first 30 sts, dividing them between 3 needles as you go, 10 sts on each needle. Place the last 30 sts on a piece of scrap yarn. Using a 4th needle, CO10 sts as the inside edge of the first leg. Pm, join the knit in the round, (see figure 2). Stuff the body before beginning knitting.
Rounds 1–5: Knit. 40 sts
Change to MC.
Rounds 6–11: Knit.
Change to CC.
Round 12: (K10, k2tog, k6, ssk) twice. 36 sts

Rounds 13–17: Knit.
Change to MC.
Round 18: (K2tog, k4) 6 times. 30 sts
Round 19: (K2tog, k3) 6 times. 24 sts
Round 20: (K2tog, k2) 6 times. 18 sts
Round 21: (K2tog, k1) 6 times. 12 sts
Round 22: K2tog 6 times. 6 sts
Break yarn, knot, pull tail into leg. Stuff leg firmly.

Reattach CC at front center to begin 2nd leg. Pick up and knit 30 sts from scrap yarn, diving between 3 needles, 10 sts on each needle. Pick up and knit 10 sts from inside of first leg. Pm, join to knit in the round, (see figure 3). Follow the same directions as for first leg, pausing to stuff fully before closing up.

Arms (knit 2)

Using MC, CO6, pm, join to knit in the round.
Round 1: Kfb 6 times. 12 sts
Round 2: Knit.
Round 3: (Kfb, k1) 6 times. 18 sts

Rounds 4–6: Knit.
Switch to CC.
Rounds 7–12: Knit.
Bind off. Stuff arms lightly.

Assembly

Sew the arms to the side of the body, using CC, (see figure 4).
Cut felt pieces using the template. Sew the mouth to the face, centering over third MC stripe. Use red thread to sew on the tongue, (see figure 5). Use white thread to sew on each tooth, (see figure 6). Attach the eyes with black thread, centering along 2nd CC stripe, (see figure 7).

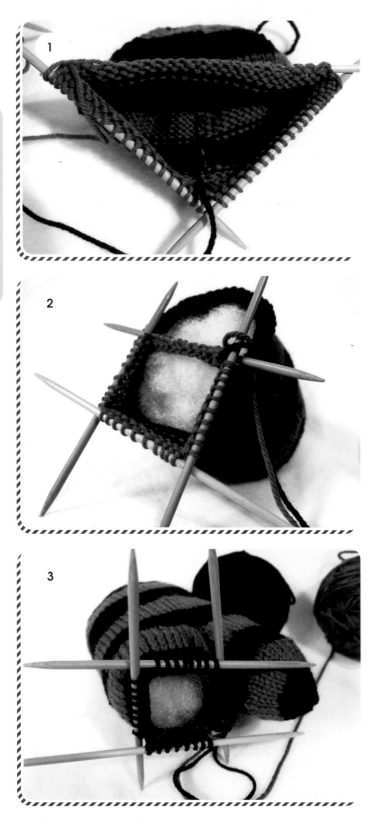

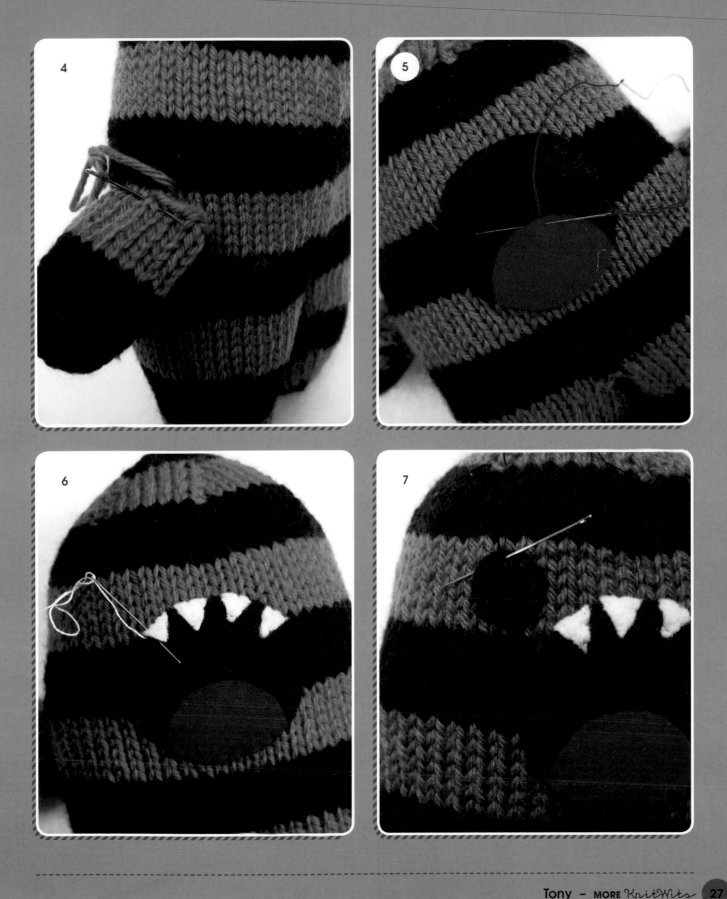

Eye (2)

Teeth

Mouth

Tongue

Pickle

When the economy started going downhill in Pickle's hometown, jobs became harder and harder to come by, particularly for a little green monster. Pickle left town in search of a better fortune. Eventually he traveled to Alaska, where he joined the crew of a fishing boat. The work was dangerous and cold, and Pickle began to think he had made a mistake. But one day his luck changed – the crew trapped another green monster in their fishing nets and pulled her into the boat. It was a lovely green lady monster, and Pickle was smitten. They soon married and settled in a cabin on the coast, raising a large family of little pickles.

Materials

- 1 skein Cascade 220 in 2409 (MC) green
- 1 skein Cascade 220 in 8892 (CC) blue
- 1 set US size 5 (3.75mm) double pointed needles
- 1 pair US size 5 (3.75mm) straight needles
- Yarn needle
- Embroidery needle
- Craft felt in blue, black, and white
- Embroidery floss in blue, black, and white
- Toy stuffing

Gauge:
22 sts and 28 rows over 4 in. in stockinette st

Finished toy size:
9 in. tall.

Glossary of abbreviations

CO	cast on
k	knit
k2tog	knit two together
kfb	knit into front and back of stitch
p	purl
pm	place marker
ssk	slip, slip, knit slipped stitches together
st[s]	stitch[es]

Body, knit from the top down

Using MC and double pointed needles, CO6, pm, join to knit in the round.
Round 1: Kfb 6 times. 12 sts
Round 2 and all even numbered rounds: Knit.
Round 3: (Kfb, k1) 6 times. 18 sts
Round 5: (Kfb, k2) 6 times. 24 sts
Round 7: (Kfb, k3) 6 times. 30 sts
Round 9: (Kfb, k4) 6 times. 36 sts
Round 10: (Kfb, k5) 6 times. 42 sts
Rounds 11–28: Knit.
Round 29: (K1, kfb, k6, kfb, k2, kfb, k7, kfb, k1) twice. 50 sts
Round 30: Knit.
Round 31: K10, kfb, k2, kfb, k9, kfb, k2, kfb, k23. 54 sts
Round 32: Knit.
Round 33: (K1, kfb, k8, kfb, k2, kfb, k11, kfb, k1) twice. 62 sts
Rounds 34–46: Knit.
Round 47: (K1, ssk, k8, k2tog, k2, ssk, k11, k2tog, k1) twice. 54 sts
Round 48: Knit.

Round 49: K10, k2tog, k2, ssk, k9, k2tog, k2, ssk, k23. 50 sts
Round 50: Knit.
Round 51: (K1, ssk, k6, k2tog, k2, ssk, k7, k2tog, k1) twice. 42 sts
Round 52: Knit.
Round 53: (K1, ssk, k4, k2tog, k12) twice. 38 sts
Round 54: Knit.
Round 55: (K1, ssk, k2, k2tog, k12) twice. 34 sts
Round 56: Knit.

Begin dividing for legs

Break yarn. Place the first 9 sts on a piece of scrap yarn. Place the next 5 sts on a double pointed needle. Place the next 12 sts on another piece of scrap yarn for second leg. Place the next 5 sts on one double pointed needle. Place the remaining 3 sts on the first piece of scrap yarn with the first 9 sts. This will be the first leg. Reconnect MC to knit the sts on one of the double pointed needles. Knit 8 rows in stockinette st, (see figure 1). Break

yarn, leaving a 12 in. tail. Use the tail and a kitchener stitch to graft the sts from the double pointed needles together. This is the crotch. Stuff body firmly.
Reconnect MC to begin first leg. Pick up and knit the 12 sts from one of the pieces of scrap yarn, dividing sts between double pointed needles. Pick up and knit 6 sts from the inside edge of the crotch. Pm, join to knit in the round. 18 sts, (see figure 2). Knit 8 rounds even.
Round 9: (K2tog, k1) 6 times. 12 sts
Round 10: K2tog 6 times. 6 sts
Break yarn, pull tail through remaining sts, knot pull tail to inside of foot. Stuff foot. Reconnect MC and knit second foot same as for first, pausing to stuff 2nd foot before closing it up.

Arms (knit 2)

Using MC and double pointed needles, CO6, pm, join to knit in the round.
Round 1: Kfb 6 times. 12 sts

Round 2: (Kfb, k1) 6 times. 18 sts
Rounds 3–6: Knit.
Round 7: (K2tog, k1) 6 times. 12 sts
Rounds 8–19: Knit.
Bind off. Stuff arms lightly. Weave in loose ends.

Hat

Using CC, CO48, pm, join to knit in the round.
Round 1: (K1, p1) 24 times.
Repeat round 1 eight more times.
Round 10: (K2tog, (k1, p1) 3 times) 6 times. 42 sts
Round 11: (K2tog, (p1, k1) twice, p1) 6 times. 36 sts
Round 12: (K2tog, k1, p1, k1, p1) 6 times. 30 sts
Round 13: (K2tog, p1, k1, p1) 6 times. 24 sts
Round 14: (K2tog, k1, p1) 6 times. 18 sts
Round 15: (K2tog, p1) 6 times. 12 sts
Round 16: K2tog 6 times.
Break yarn, pull tail through remaining sts. Weave in loose ends.

Scarf

Using CC and straight needles, CO7.
Row 1: (K1, p1) 6 times, k1.
Repeat this row until the scarf is 17 in. long.

Assembly

Using MC, sew the arms to the sides of the body, (see figure 3).
To make the pompom for the hat, wrap a piece of scrap yarn around 2 fingers 8 or 9 times, (see figure 4). Pull the loops off your fingers, and tie a strand of thread around the center, pulling tight and securing with a knot, (see figure 5). Cut the ends of loops, and trim the ends until the pompom is round and desired size. Use the thread to secure the pompom to the top of the hat.
Cut the eyes using templates. Sew to the face using the same color of thread, (see figure 6). Place the hat and the scarf on the monster.

4

Eyeball (3) Iris (3) Pupil (3)

5

HMMFH
FNUFFLE FUNF
NFFLE MFFLE!

6

Mac

It's quite embarrassing to live with a large bite taken out of the side of your head. Mac has never really come to terms with it. Never mind that he's a magnificently shiny, red apple, when Mac looks in the mirror, he only sees that singular flaw. He's vowed to seek revenge on the poor fool who inflicted the wound. Think of Mac the next time you're tempted to eat an apple.

Materials

- 1 skein Cascade 220 in 8895 (MC) red
- 1 skein Cascade 220 in 8894 (CC) green
- 1 set US size 5 (3.75mm) double pointed knitting needles
- Small amount of brown yarn
- Felt in black, blue, and white
- Embroidery floss in black, blue, and white
- Yarn needle
- Embroidery needle
- Toy stuffing

Gauge:
22 sts and 28 rows over 4 in. in stockinette st

Finished toy size:
6 in. tall.

Glossary of abbreviations

CO	cast on
k	knit
k2tog	knit two together
kfb	knit into front and back of stitch
pm	place marker
ssk	slip, slip, knit slipped stitches together
st[s]	stitch[es]

Body, knit from the bottom up
Base (knit 2)
Using MC, CO8, pm, join to knit in the round.
Round 1: (K1, kfb twice, k1) twice. 12 sts
Round 2: (K1, kfb, k2, kfb, k1) twice. 16 sts
Break yarn. Leave sts on needles or scrap yarn. Using remaining needles, cast on again and repeat rounds 1 and 2.
Place both pieces of base side by side on two double pointed needles. Reconnect MC at one side, pm, begin knitting in the round. 32 sts, (see figure 1).
Round 1: (K1, kfb, k12, kfb, k1) twice. 36 sts
Round 2: (K1, kfb, k14, kfb, k1) twice. 40 sts
Round 3: Knit.
Round 4: (K1, kfb, k16, kfb, k1) twice. 44 sts
Round 5–6: Knit.
Round 7: (K1, kfb, k18, kfb, k1) twice. 48 sts
Round 8–9: Knit.
Round 10: (K1, kfb, k20, kfb, k1) twice.

52 sts
Rounds 11–18: Knit.
Round 19: (K1, kfb, k22, kfb, k1) twice. 56 sts
Rounds 20–22: Knit.
Round 23: Ssk, k52, k2tog. 54 sts
Round 24: Ssk, k50, k2tog. 52 sts
Round 25: ssk, k48, k2tog. 50 sts
Round 26: Knit.
Round 27: Kfb, k48, kfb. 52 sts
Round 28: Knit.
Round 29: Ssk, k48, k2tog. 50 sts
Round 30: Ssk, k46, k2tog. 48 sts
Round 31: Ssk, k44, k2tog. 46 sts
Round 32: K20, k2tog, k2, ssk, k20. 44 sts
Round 33: Kfb, k42, kfb. 46 sts
Round 34: Kfb, k19, k2tog, k2, ssk, k19, kfb.

Begin splitting for top of apple
K8, k2tog, k1, move the next 24 sts to a piece of scrap yarn, k1, ssk, k8. 20 sts
Continue knitting right upper section of apple:
Round 1: (K1, ssk, k4, k2tog, k1) twice. 16 sts

Round 2: (K1, ssk, k2, k2tog, k1) twice. 12 sts
Round 3: (K1, ssk, k2tog, k1) twice. 8 sts
Bind off. Use tail to sew small hole closed. Use MC to close up holes at bottom. Stuff apple.
Return sts from scrap yarn to two double pointed needles, 12 sts per needle. Reattach MC at edge, (see figure 2). 24 sts
Round 1: (K1, ssk, k6, k2tog, k1) twice. 20 sts
Round 2: (K1, ssk, k4, k2tog, k1) twice. 16 sts
Round 3: (K1, ssk, k2, k2tog, k1) twice. 12 sts
Bind off. Stuff apple full. Use tail to seam hole closed.

Leaf
Using CC, CO4, pm, join to knit in the round.
Round 1: Kfb 4 times. 8 sts
Round 2 and all even rounds: Knit.
Round 3: (K1, kfb twice, k1) twice. 12 sts
Round 5: (K1, kfb, k2, kfb, k1) twice. 16 sts

Round 7: (K1, kfb, k4, kfb, k1) twice.
20 sts
Rounds 8–10: Knit.
Round 11: (K1, ssk, k4, k2tog, k1) twice.
16 sts
Round 13: (K1, ssk, k2, k2tog, k1) twice.
12 sts
Round 15: (K1, ssk, k2tog, k1) twice. 8 sts
Round 17: (Ssk, k2tog) twice. 4 sts
Break yarn, pull tail through remaining sts.
Do not stuff. Pull tail to inside of leaf.

Stem
Using brown yarn, CO3. Knit a 1 in. i-cord.
Bind off.

Assembly

Using tail, sew the stem to the top center
of the apple, (see figure 3). Sew the leaf
to the side of the stem, (see figure 4).
Cut all felt pieces using template. Sew
the eyes to the face using a matching
color of embroidery floss, (see figure 5).
Use a full thickness of black embroidery
floss to line the tops of the eyes, and to
create a down-turned mouth by running
a length across the top of the fabric,
and securing into place using a separate
single strand, (see figure 6).

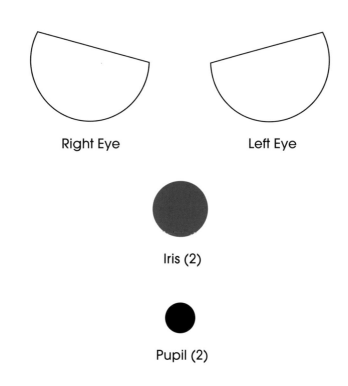

Right Eye   Left Eye

Iris (2)

Pupil (2)

Grapefruit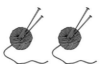

You may think Grapefruit was born with her lovely spots, but in reality, they are merely the result of messy eating. Her favorite food is, of course, banana pudding. Unfortunately, 80% of the pudding she scoops up with her spoon, winds up on her pelt. In addition, Grapefruit is often so busy eating, that she frequently forgets to bathe. Her parents were embarrassed by their daughter's table manners, exhausted from the daily scrubbing, and broke from the extensive dry cleaning bills. Eventually they gave up, and began telling their friends and extended family that the spots are natural.

Materials

- 1 skein Cascade 220 in 2436 (MC)
- 1 skein Cascade 220 in 8010 (CC)
- 1 pair US size 6 (4.00mm) straight needles
- 1 set US size 6 (4.00mm) double pointed needles
- Two ½ in. circles cut from black felt for eyes
- Embroidery floss in black
- Yarn needle
- Embroidery needle
- Toy stuffing

Gauge:
20 sts and 26 rows over 4 in. in stockinette st

Finished toy size:
10½ in. tall.

Glossary of abbreviations

CO	cast on
k	knit
k2tog	knit two together
kfb	knit into front and back of stitch
pm	place marker
ssk	slip, slip, knit slipped stitches together
st[s]	stitch[es]

Body, knit from the bottom up (Knit 2)
Using straight needles and MC, CO18 sts.
Row 1: K1, kfb, k14, kfb, k1. 20 sts
Row 2: Purl.
Row 3: K1, kfb, k16, kfb, k1. 22 sts
Row 4: Purl.
Row 5: K1, kfb, k18, kfb, k1. 24 sts
Row 6: Purl.
Begin knitting chart, starting with a knit row, continuing in stockinette st. When changing colors, be sure to twist sts, to avoid creating a small hole in the fabric. Do not run colors behind the fabric, as doing so will prevent the fabric from stretching easily when stuffing toy. Instead, wind bobbins of each color, (see figure 1).
After completing chart, continue knitting as follows:
Rows 46–49: Complete evenly in stockinette st.
Row 50: K1, k2tog, k18, ssk, k1. 22 sts
Row 51: Purl.

Row 52: K1, k2tog, k16, ssk, k1. 20 sts
Row 53: Purl.
Row 54: K1, k2tog, k14, ssk, k1. 18 sts
Bind off, leaving a 30 in. tail for seaming.
Block front and back.

Feet (knit 2)
Using double pointed needles and MC, CO6, pm, join to knit in the round.
Round 1: (Kfb, k1, kfb) twice. 10 sts
Round 2: Knit.
Round 3: (Kfb, k3, kfb) twice. 14 sts
Rounds 4–5: Knit.
Round 6: (K2tog, k2, ssk) twice. 10 sts
Rounds 7–9: Knit.
Bind off, leaving a 6 in. tail for seaming.

Arms (knit 2)
Using double pointed needles and MC, CO6, pm, join to knit in the round.
Round 1: (Kfb, k1, kfb) twice. 10 sts
Rounds 2–4: Knit.
Round 5: K2tog, k1, ssk) twice. 6 sts
Knit 6 rounds evenly. Bind off, leaving a 6 in. tail for seaming.

Horns (knit 2)
Using double pointed needles and MC, CO4.
Knit a 1 in. i-cord, then continue as follows:
(K1, kfb) twice. 6 sts
Knit 3 more rounds as an i-cord. Break yarn, pull tail through remaining sts, knot, pull knot to inside of horn.

Assembly

Weave in the loose ends. Seam together the front and back using tail of yarn, matching polka dots at the sides, (see figure 2). Pause after sewing three sides to stuff the body. Press flat to get shape pushing stuffing into the corners. Be careful not to overstuff.

Stuff the legs very lightly. The arms and horns are not stuffed. Sew on the legs, arms and horns, (see figure 3). Use a full thickness of embroidery floss to create a smile. Use a single strand to sew over the smile and hold it in place (outline stitch), (see figure 4). Use a single strand of embroidery floss to secure felt eyes in place, (see figure 5).

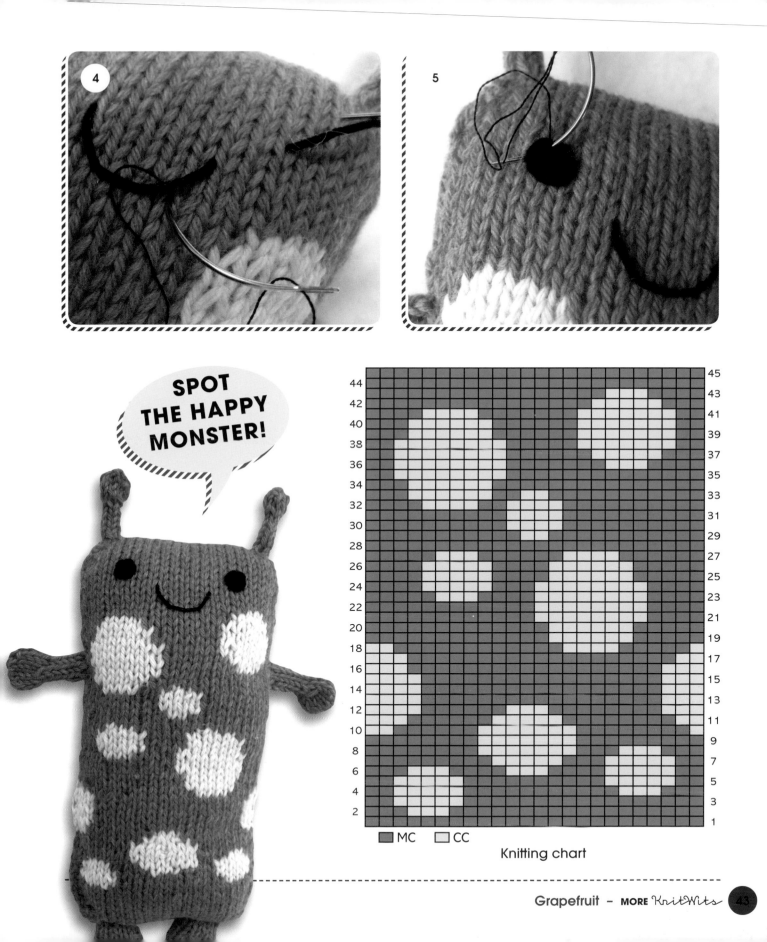

SPOT THE HAPPY MONSTER!

44 · 42 · 40 · 38 · 36 · 34 · 32 · 30 · 28 · 26 · 24 · 22 · 20 · 18 · 16 · 14 · 12 · 10 · 8 · 6 · 4 · 2

45 · 43 · 41 · 39 · 37 · 35 · 33 · 31 · 29 · 27 · 25 · 23 · 21 · 19 · 17 · 15 · 13 · 11 · 9 · 7 · 5 · 3 · 1

■ MC   □ CC

Knitting chart

Boris

Boris is a very lazy little monster. He's never cared much for sports or exercise, so he was very upset to learn one summer that his parents had decided to move to the city, into a 9th story apartment in a building with no elevator. Boris would take his time walking up that long flight of stairs. Everyday he'd walk home from school and begin his climb. By the 3rd floor he'd have to stop for a drink of water. By the 5th floor it was time for a snack break. And by the time Boris had reached the 7th floor, he would stop and take a very long nap. It took Boris so long to climb the stairs that he would often miss dinner. Finally his mother, fed up with eating dinner near midnight, came up with a solution. And so Boris came to have his bright red balloon. The balloon wasn't merely to amuse him, but rather to carry him up, up, up, all the way to the 9th floor.

Materials

- 1 skein Cascade 220 in 8892 (MC) blue
- 1 skein Cascade 220 in 8505 (CC1) white
- 1 skein Cascade 220 in 8686 (CC2) brown
- 1 skein Cascade 220 in 8895 (CC3) red
- 1 set US size 6 (4.00mm) double pointed needles
- Yarn needle
- Embroidery needle
- Craft felt in black, white, and blue
- Embroidery floss in black, white, blue, and red
- Toy stuffing
- 1 small black coffee stirring straw
- 2 cotton swabs

Gauge:
20 sts and 26 rows over 4 in. in stockinette st

Finished toy size:
11½ in. tall.

Glossary of abbreviations

CO	cast on
k	knit
k2tog	knit two together
kfb	knit into front and back of stitch
p	purl
pm	place marker
ssk	slip, slip, knit slipped stitches together
st[s]	stitch[es]

Body, knit from the top down.
Using MC, CO6, pm, join to knit in the round.
Round 1: Kfb 6 times. 12 sts
Round 2: (Kfb, k1) 6 times. 18 sts
Round 3: Knit.
Round 4: (Kfb, k2) 6 times. 24 sts
Round 5: Knit.
Round 6: (Kfb, k3) 6 times. 30 sts
Round 7: Knit.
Round 8: (Kfb, k4) 6 times. 36 sts
Rounds 9: Knit.
Round 10: (Kfb, k5) 6 times. 42 sts
Rounds 11–22: Knit.
Round 23: (K2tog, k5) 6 times. 36 sts
Rounds 24–29: Knit.
Round 30: (Kfb, k5) 6 times. 42 sts
Rounds 31–33: Knit.
Switch to CC1.

Rounds 34–42: Knit.
Round 43: K5, kfb, k9, kfb, k10, kfb, k9, kfb, k5. 46 sts
Round 44: Knit.
Round 45: K17, kfb, k10, kfb, k17. 48 sts
Round 46: Knit.
Round 47: K6, kfb, k9, kfb, k3, kfb, k6, kfb, k3, kfb, k9, kfb, k6. 54 sts
Round 48: Knit.
Round 49: K22, kfb, k8, kfb, k22. 56 sts
Switch to MC.
Round 50: Knit.
Round 51: K7, kfb, k9, kfb, k6, kfb, k6, kfb, k6, kfb, k9, kfb, k7. 62 sts
Round 52: Knit.
Round 53: K27, kfb, k6, kfb, k27. 64 sts
Rounds 54–55: Knit.
Switch to CC2.
Round 56: K27, ssk, k6, k2tog, k27. 62 sts

Round 57: K7, k2tog, k9, ssk, k6, k2tog, k6, ssk, k6, k2tog, k9, ssk, k7. 56 sts
Round 58: K22, k2tog, k8, ssk, k22. 54 sts
Round 59: K6, k2tog, k9, ssk, k2, k2tog, k8, ssk, k2, k2tog, k9, ssk, k6. 48 sts
Round 60: K17, k2tog, k10, ssk, k17. 46 sts
Round 61: K5, k2tog, k9, ssk, k10, k2tog, k9, ssk, k5. 42 sts
Round 62: Knit.
Round 63: (K2tog, k5) 6 times. 36 sts
Round 64: Knit.

Begin dividing for legs
Knit the first 18 sts, dividing them between 3 needles as you go, 6 sts on each needle.
Place the last 18 sts on a piece of scrap yarn. Using a 4th needle, CO6 sts as the inside edge of the first leg. Pm, join to knit in the round, (see figure 1). Stuff the

body before beginning knitting.
Rounds 1–9: Knit. 24 sts
Round 10: (K2tog, k2) 6 times. 18 sts
Round 11: Knit.
Round 12: (K2tog, k1) 6 times. 12 sts
Round 13: K2tog 6 times. 6 sts
Break yarn, pull tail through remaining sts, knot, pull tail to inside of toy.
Stuff knitted leg. Reattach yarn between legs. Knit the 18 sts from the scrap yarn, dividing between 3 needles, 6 sts per needle. With a 4th needle, pick up and knit 6 sts from the inside edge of the first leg. Pm, join to knit in the round. Follow the directions as for first leg, pausing near the end to stuff leg before closing up sts.

Arms (knit 2)
Using CC1, CO5, pm, join to knit in the round.
Round 1: Kfb 5 times. 10 sts
Round 2: (Kfb, k1) 5 times. 15 sts
Rounds 3–7: Knit.
Switch to MC.
Round 8: Knit.
Round 9: (Kfb, k4) 3 times. 18 sts
Rounds 10–19: Knit.
Round 20: (K2tog, k1) 6 times. 12 sts
Round 21: K2tog 6 times.
Break yarn, pull tail through remaining sts, knot, pull tail to inside of arm.

Balloon
Using CC3, CO6, pm, join top knit in the round.

Round 1: Kfb 6 times. 12 sts
Round 2 and all even numbered rounds: Knit.
Round 3: (Kfb, k1) 6 times. 18 sts
Round 5: (Kfb, k2) 6 times. 24 sts
Round 7: (Kfb, k3) 6 times. 30 sts
Round 9: (Kfb, k4) 6 times. 36 sts
Rounds 10–16: Knit.
Round 17: (K2tog, k4) 6 times. 30 sts
Rounds 18–19: Knit.
Round 20: (K2tog, k3) 6 times. 24 sts
Rounds 21–22: Knit.
Pause to stuff balloon mostly full.
Round 23: (K2tog, k2) 6 times. 18 sts
Rounds 24–25: Knit.
Round 26: (K2tog, k1) 6 times. 12 sts
Stuff balloon firmly.
Round 27: K2tog 6 times. Bind off.

Assembly

Stuff the arms firmly. Seam to the sides of the body, with one arm down, and one pointed outwards to hold the balloon, (see figure 2).
Cut felt pieces using the template. Attach the eyes to the face, using the corresponding color of thread, (see figure 3). Use a full thickness of black embroidery floss to create the smile and the bottom outline of the eye. Sew hair to the top of the head with red thread.
For the balloon, cut a long strand of red thread and run through center of stirring stick with an embroidery needle, (see figure 4). Run the needle straight through the hole in the bottom of the balloon, and through the top, inserting the stick well into the balloon, (see figure 5). Place the balloon in his hand, sewing into place with the other end of the red thread. Fold the hand over and sew into place using MC yarn, (see figure 6). If extra stability is needed, cut the cotton tips off the swabs. Insert into the fabric through the back of the body into the arm, pushing them in until the ends of swabs are absorbed into the fabric of the toy.

1

Hair

Eyeball

Iris

Pupil

Hot Rod

Now I know what you're thinking, but you're wrong. It's not Botox. Hot Rod's lips really are that big naturally. Some fish are just born lucky. Hot Rod never had a problem finding a mate . . . or three. He was quite the Casanova. What lady fish wouldn't want to kiss Hot Rod? But being so well endowed has its drawbacks. A fish with big lips is just that much easier to hook. Little did he know the fisherman that caught Hot Rod left behind an ocean full of broken hearts.

Materials

- 1 skein Cascade 220 in 2436 (MC)
- 1 skein Cascade 220 in 7824 (CC)
- Small amount of worsted weight yarn in white for eyes
- 1 set US size 6 (4.00mm) double pointed needles
- Scrap of black felt
- Toy stuffing
- Yarn needle
- Embroidery needle
- Embroidery floss in black

Gauge:
20 sts and 26 rows over 4 in. in stockinette st

Finished toy size:
9½ in. tall.

Glossary of abbreviations

CO	cast on
k	knit
k2tog	knit two together
kfb	knit into front and back of stitch
p	purl
pm	place marker
ssk	slip, slip, knit slipped stitches together
st[s]	stitch[es]
w&t	wrap and turn

Hot Rod is knitted much like a sock, and uses short shaping to turn the head, just as you would turn a heel.

Head, starting with the mouth
Using double pointed needles and MC, CO16, pm, join to knit in the round.
Round 1: (K1, kfb, k4, kfb, k1) twice. 20 sts
Round 2: (K1, kfb, k6, kfb, k1) twice. 24 sts
Round 3: (K1, kfb, k8, kfb, k1) twice. 28 sts
Round 4: (K1, kfb, k10, kfb, k1) twice. 32 sts
Round 5: (K1, kfb, k12, kfb, k1) twice. 36 sts
Round 6: (K1, kfb, k14, kfb, k1) twice. 40 sts
Round 7: (K1, kfb, k16, kfb, k1) twice. 44 sts
Round 8: (K1, kfb, k18, kfb, k1) twice. 48 sts
Rounds 9–22: Knit.
Begin short row shaping for neck. Be sure to leave stitch marker in place:
Row 23: K23, w&t.
Row 24: P22, w&t.
Row 25: K21, w&t.
Row 26: P20, w&t.
Row 27: K19, w&t.
Row 28: P18, w&t.
Row 29: K17, w&t.
Row 30: P16, w&t.
Row 31: K15, w&t.
Row 32: P14, w&t.
Row 33: K13, w&t.
Row 34: P12, w&t.
Row 35: K11, w&t.
Row 36: P10, w&t.
Row 37: K10, on the next stitch, insert the tip of needle through the wrap under the stitch, and then the stitch itself and knit them together, (see figure 1), w&t the next stitch.
Row 38: P11, on the next stitch, pick up the wrapped stitch from the front, place it on the needle, and purl it together with the first stitch, w&t the next stitch.
Row 39: K12, on the next stitch, pick up BOTH of the wrapped stitches from the front, place them on the needle, and purl them together with the first stitch, w&t the next stitch.
Row 40: P13, on the next stitch, pick up BOTH of the wrapped stitches from the front, place them on the needle next to the first, and purl the three of them together, (see figure 2), w&t the next stitch.
Continue in this manner, increasing the number of stitches worked by one each row, and picking up wraps, until you have picked up all wrapped sts. W&t the next stitch, and then knit back around to the stitch marker.
Return to knitting in the round to continue body.

Body
Rounds 1–5: Knit. 48 sts
Round 6: (K1, ssk, k18, k2tog, k1) twice. 44 sts
Rounds 7–8: Knit.
Round 9: (K1, ssk, k16, k2tog, k1) twice.

40 sts

Rounds 10–11: Knit.

Round 12: (K1, ssk, k14, k2tog, k1) twice. 36 sts

Rounds 13–14: Knit.

Round 15: (K1, ssk, k3, ssk, k2, k2tog, k3, k2tog, k1) twice. 28 sts

Rounds 16–30: Knit.

Stuff body mostly full.

Round 31: (K1, ssk, k8, k2tog, k1) twice. 24 sts

Round 32: Knit.

Round 33: (K1, ssk, k6, k2tog, k1) twice. 20 sts

Round 34: Knit.

Round 35: (K1, ssk, k4, k2tog, k1) twice. 16 sts

Round 36: Knit.

Stuff rest of body.

Switch to CC and begin tail:

Round 1: (K1, kfb, k4, kfb, k1) twice. 20 sts

Round 2: (K1, kfb, k6, kfb, k1) twice. 24 sts

Round 3: (K1, kfb, k8, kfb, k1) twice. 28 sts

Begin dividing for fins

Round 4: Using a double pointed needle, k1, kfb, k5, place the next 7 sts on a 2nd double pointed needle, place the next 7 sts on a 3rd double pointed needle, using the 4th needle, k5, kfb, k1.

Round 5: K1, kfb, k6, take yarn through middle of tail and begin knitting sts on 4th needle, k6, kfb, k1. 18 sts (on left fin). Continue knitting these sts as follows, (see figure 3).

*Round 6: K1, kfb, k5, ssk, k2tog, k5, kfb, k1.

Round 7: K1, kfb, k14, kfb, k1. 20 sts

Round 8: K1, kfb, k6, ssk, k2tog, k6, kfb, k1.

Round 9: K1, kfb, k16, kfb, k1. 22 sts

Round 10: K1, kfb, k7, ssk, k2tog, k7, kfb, k1.

Round 11: K1, kfb, k18, kfb, k1. 24 sts

Round 12: K1, kfb, k8, ssk, k2tog, k8, kfb, k1.

Round 13: Knit.

Round 14: K1, kfb, k8, ssk, k2tog, k8,

kfb, k1.

Round 15: K10, ssk, k2tog, k10. 22 sts

Round 16: K9, ssk, k2tog, k9. 20 sts

Round 17: K8, ssk, k2tog, k8. 18 sts

Round 18: K7, ssk, k2tog, k7. 16 sts

Round 19: K6, ssk, k2tog, k6. 14 sts

Round 20: K5, ssk, k2tog, k5. 12 sts

Round 21: K4, ssk, k2tog, k4. 10 sts

Round 22: K3, ssk, k2tog, k3. 8 sts

Round 23: K2tog 4 times. 4 sts

Break yarn, pull tail through remaining sts, knot, pull to inside of fin.

Reattach CC yarn to outside edge of remaining needles to begin right fin.

Begin as follows: K1, kfb, k10, kfb, k1. 16 sts

Next round: K1, kfb, k12, kfb, k1. 18 sts

Beginning from the (*) knit same as for directions for left fin.

Stuff head. Seam opening closed.

Bottom lip

The lips are completed in reverse stockinette, beginning with a purl row. Make certain you are picking up from the correct edge. Using CC and double pointed needles, pick up from the fish's right side and purl 24 sts across center of mouth, (see figure 4).

Row 1: S1, k23.

Row 2: S1, p19, w&t.

Row 3: K16, w&t.

Row 4: P12, w&t.

Row 5: K8, w&t.

Row 6: P16.

Bind off knitwise. Weave in loose end. Lip will curl over.

Top lip

Using CC and beginning from the fish's left side of face, pick up and purl 24 sts along the inside edge of the bottom lip, (see figure 5). Turn and follow directions same as for bottom lip.

Side fins (knit 2)

Using CC and double pointed needles, CO12, pm, join to knit in the round.

Round 1: (K1, kfb, k2, kfb, k1) twice. 16 sts

Round 2 and every even numbered round: Knit.

Round 3: (K1, kfb, k4, kfb, k1) twice. 20 sts

Round 5: (K1, kfb, k6, kfb, k1) twice. 24 sts

Rounds 6–8: Knit.

Round 9: (K1, ssk, k6, k2tog, k1) twice. 20 sts

Round 11: (K1, ssk, k4, k2tog, k1) twice. 16 sts

Round 13: (K1, ssk, k2, k2tog, k1) twice. 12 sts

Round 15: K2tog 6 times. 6 sts

Break yarn, pull tail through remaining sts, knot, pull to inside of fin.

Eyes (knit 2)

Using white yarn and double pointed needles, CO6, pm, join to knit in the round.

Round 1: Kfb 6 times. 12 sts

Round 2: (Kfb, k1) 6 times. 18 sts

Knit 5 rounds. Bind off.

Assembly

Seam the side fins to the body, (see figure 6).

Seam the eyes to the top of the head, pausing when 2/3rds of the way done to stuff eyes firmly, (see figure 7).

Use a full thickness of black embroidery floss to sew a straight line across center of the lips.

Sew the pupils to the eyeballs using black thread, (see figure 8).

Matilda

Everyone knows there are cute bugs, like ladybugs for instance. And then there are ugly bugs, like Madagascar hissing cockroaches. Matilda fortunately falls into the first category. She doesn't hiss, bite, or sting. She will, however, happily eat those lovely, plump homegrown tomatoes you have in your backyard. Matilda has a voracious appetite, and the harder you work on your garden, the more likely she is to enjoy it. How do you think she got so big for a bug? Being so very large and so very fuchsia, you might wonder how her species has survived at all, pillaging gardens in plain sight. The answer lies in her cuteness. Matilda's species evolved in a way that made it very hard for people to squash her. Look into her big sparkly eyes, and you might just put down your shovel.

Materials

- 1 skein Cascade 128 chunky in 7802 (MC)
- Small amount of worsted weight black yarn for antennae
- 1 set US size 10 (6.00mm) double pointed needles
- 1 set US size 6 (4.00mm) double pointed needles
- Pieces of wool felt in white, black, and purple
- Toy stuffing
- Yarn needle
- Embroidery needle
- Embroidery floss in white, black, and purple
- Baking soda (for felting)

Gauge:
16 sts and 20 rows
over 4 in. in stockinette st

Finished toy size:
Before felting: 12 in. tall
After felting 8 in. tall

Glossary of abbreviations

CO	cast on
k	knit
k2tog	knit two together
kfb	knit into front and back of stitch
p	purl
pm	place marker
ssk	slip, slip, knit slipped stitches together
st[s]	stitch[es]

Matilda is knitted, assembled, and then felted to give her that fuzzy round appearance.

Body
Using US size 10 (6.00mm) double pointed needles and MC, CO6, pm, join to knit in the round.
Round 1: Kfb 6 times. 12 sts
Round 2: (Kfb, k1) 6 times. 18 sts
Round 3: (K1, kfb, k5, kfb, k1) twice. 22 sts
Round 4: (K1, kfb, k7, kfb, k1) twice. 26 sts
Round 5: (K1, kfb, k9, kfb, k1) twice. 30 sts
Round 6: (K1, kfb, k11, kfb, k1) twice. 34 sts
Round 7 and all odd rounds through round 49: Knit.
Round 8: (K1, kfb, k13, kfb, k1) twice. 38 sts
Round 10: (K1, kfb, k15, kfb, k1) twice. 42 sts
Round 12: (K1, kfb, k17, kfb, k1) twice. 46 sts
Round 14: (K1, kfb, k19, kfb, k1) twice. 50 sts
Rounds 15–43: Knit.
Round 44: (K1, k2tog, k19, ssk, k1) twice. 46 sts
Round 46: (K1, k2tog, k17, ssk, k1) twice. 42 sts
Round 48: (K1, k2tog, k15, ssk, k1) twice. 38 sts
Round 50: (K1, k2tog, k13, ssk, k1) twice. 34 sts
Round 51: (K1, k2tog, k11, ssk, k1) twice. 30 sts
Round 52: (K1, k2tog, k9, ssk, k1) twice. 26 sts
Round 53: (K1, k2tog, k7, ssk, k1) twice. 22 sts
Bind off, leaving an 18 in. tail for seaming.

Stuff very lightly. The toy will shrink to the stuffing during the felting process. Seam opening closed. Weave in loose ends.

Legs (knit 2)
Using US size 10 (6.00mm) double pointed needles and MC CO6, pm, join to knit in the round.
Round 1: Kfb 6times. 12 sts
Round 2: (Kfb, k1) 6 times. 18 sts
Rounds 3–11: Knit.
Bind off, leaving a 12 in. tail for seaming. Stuff very lightly.

Arms (knit 4)
Using US size 10 (6.00mm) double pointed needles and MC CO6, pm, join to knit in the round.
Round 1: Kfb 6times. 12 sts
Rounds 2–5: Knit.
Round 6: K2tog 6 times. 6 sts
Rounds 7–8: Knit.

Bind off, leaving a 10 in. tail for seaming. Stuff very lightly.

Antennae (make 2)

Using US size 6 (4.00mm) double pointed needles and black yarn, CO4, joint to knit an i-cord.

Knit the i-cord for 1½ in., and begin increasing.

Round 1: (Kfb, k1) twice. 6 sts

Round 2: (Kfb, k2) twice. 8 sts

Rounds 3–4: Knit.

Round 5: K2tog 4 times.

Cut yarn, pull tail through remaining sts. Knot, pull yarn to inside of antennae.

Assembly

Sew the legs to the bottom of the body. Sew the arms to side of the body, (see figure 1). The body is ready for felting, (see figure 2).

Felting

You can felt the body by hand or in a top loading washing machine. I used the washing machine. Fill the washer to the lowest water setting with hot water. Add 2 tbsp baking soda. Drop the toy in and run through the agitation cycle. Stop every 10 minutes to check progress, and squeeze water from the toy. Reset the cycle as needed without draining the washer.

I felted mine for 40 minutes. When the toy is 8 in. from the top of the head to the bottom of the feet, drain the water, and allow the toy to run through the rinse cycle. Remove before the final spin cycle. Squeeze out as much water as possible, and shape the toy as needed. Place the toy in a warm spot to dry completely. The felted body should look like this: (see figure 3).

Once the toy is dry, you can add the embellishments.

Antennae

If your antenna is too floppy, you can cut a pipe cleaner or cotton swab to the correct length and insert. Seam to the top of the head, (see figure 4).

Cut felt pieces using the template. Use purple thread to attach the belly to the front, (see figure 5).

Use white and black thread to sew the eyes to the face. Use white thread to create reflections in the eyes, (see figure 6).

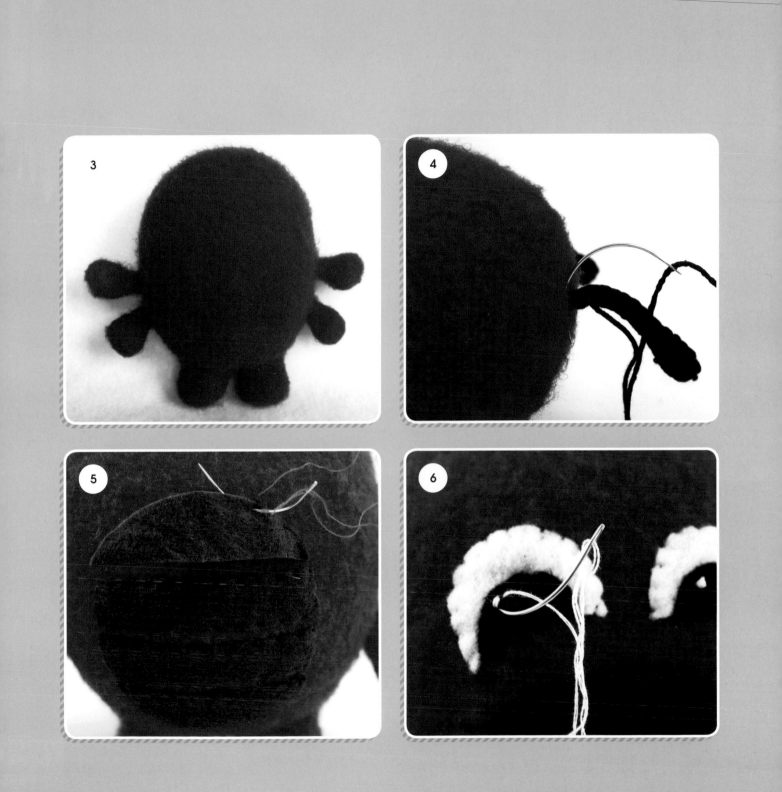

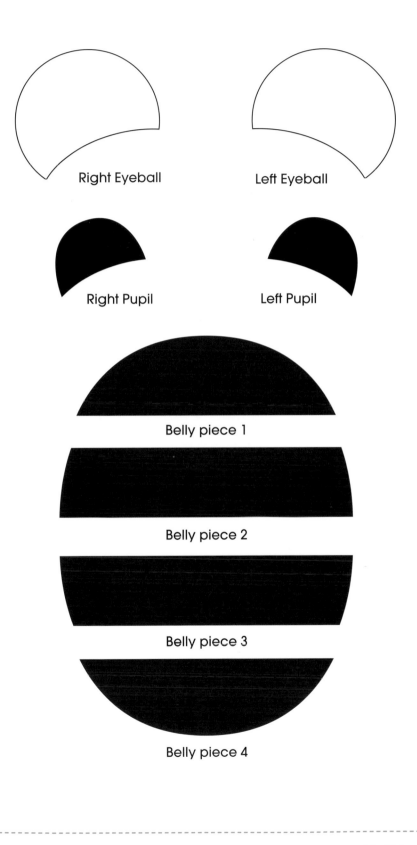

Right Eyeball

Left Eyeball

Right Pupil

Left Pupil

Belly piece 1

Belly piece 2

Belly piece 3

Belly piece 4

Fireball

Flying should come naturally to a dragon, but not to Fireball. Despite having a very nice pair of little green wings, Fireball simply could not get off the ground. But the problem wasn't with his wings. Fireball couldn't lift off because of his disproportionately large and round belly. Perhaps he's eaten too many cheeseburgers (cheeseburgers being the favorite food of all dragons). It's embarrassing to be a flightless dragon, so Fireball tried every way he could possibly think of to drop the extra weight. When the latest fad diets did nothing to improve his waistline, he reluctantly turned to exercise. Surprisingly enough, Fireball turned out to be an excellent cyclist. Now a much slimmer dragon, Fireball can fly as well as any of his friends, but he still prefers traveling by bicycle.

Materials

- 1 skein Cascade 220 in 8893 (MC)
- 1 skein Cascade 220 in 9461 (CC)
- 1 set US size 6 (4.00mm) double pointed needles
- 1 pair US size 6 (4.00mm) straight needles
- Yarn needle
- Embroidery needle
- Craft felt in light green, black and white
- Embroidery floss in light green, black and white
- Toy stuffing

Gauge:
20 sts and 26 rows over 4 in. in stockinette st

Finished toy size:
11½ in. tall.

Glossary of abbreviations

CO	cast on
k	knit
k2tog	knit two together
kfb	knit into front and back of stitch
p	purl
pm	place marker
ssk	slip, slip, knit slipped stitches together
st[s]	stitch[es]

Body, knit from the shoulders down
Using MC and double pointed needles, CO28, pm, join to knit in the round.
Round 1: (Kfb, k4, kfb, k8) twice. 32 sts
Round 2: (Kfb, k6, kfb, k8) twice. 36 sts
Round 3: (Kfb, k8, kfb, k8) twice. 40 sts
Round 4: (Kfb, k10, kfb, k8) twice. 44 sts
Round 5: (Kfb, k12, kfb, k8) twice. 48 sts
Rounds 6–14: Knit.
Round 15: Kfb, k14, kfb twice, k30, kfb. 52 sts
Round 16: Kfb, k16, kfb twice, k32, kfb. 56 sts
Round 17: Kfb, k18, kfb twice, k34, kfb. 60 sts
Round 18: Kfb, k20, kfb twice, k36, kfb. 64 sts
Rounds 19–20: Knit.
Round 21: K42, kfb, k2, kfb, k18. 66 sts
Rounds 22–23: Knit.
Round 24: K43, kfb, k2, kfb, k19. 68 sts
Rounds 25–36: Knit.
Round 37: Ssk, k20, k2tog, ssk, k40, k2tog. 64 sts
Round 38: Ssk, k18, k2tog, ssk, k38, k2tog. 60 sts
Round 39: Ssk, k16, k2tog, ssk, k36, k2tog. 56 sts
Round 40: Ssk, k14, k2tog, ssk, k32, k2tog. 52 sts
Round 41: Ssk, k12, k2tog, ssk, k30, k2tog. 48 sts
Round 42: Ssk, k10, k2tog, ssk, k28, k2tog. 44 sts
Round 43: Ssk, k8, k2tog, ssk, k26, k2tog. 40 sts
Round 44: Ssk, k6, k2tog, ssk, k24, k2tog. 36 sts
Round 45: (K2tog, k4) 6 times. 30 sts
Round 46: (K2tog, k3) 6 times. 24 sts
Round 47: (K2tog, k2) 6 times. 18 sts
Round 48: (K2tog, k1) 6 times. 12 sts
Round 49: K2tog 6 times. 6 sts
Break yarn, pull tail through remaining sts, knot, pull knot to inside of body.

Head
Using MC and double pointed needles, CO6, pm, join to knit in the round.
Round 1: Kfb 6 times. 12 sts
Round 2 and all even numbered rounds through round 10: Knit.
Round 3: (Kfb, k1) 6 times. 18 sts
Round 5: (Kfb, k2) 6 times. 24 sts
Round 7: (Kfb, k3) 6 times. 30 sts
Round 9: (Kfb, k4) 6 times. 36 sts
Round 11: (Kfb, k5) 6 times. 42 sts
Rounds 12–15: Knit.
Round 16: K6, kfb twice, k12, kfb twice, k20. 46 sts
Round 17: K7, kfb twice, k14, kfb twice, k21. 50 sts
Round 18: K8, kfb twice, k16, kfb twice, k22. 54 sts
Round 19: K9, kfb twice, k18, kfb twice, k23. 58 sts
Round 20: K10, kfb twice, k20, kfb twice, k24. 62 sts

Round 21–29: Knit.
Round 30: K10, k2tog, ssk, k20, k2tog, ssk, k24. 58 sts
Round 31: K9, k2tog, ssk, k18, k2tog, ssk, k23. 54 sts
Round 32: K8, k2tog, ssk, k16, k2tog, ssk, k22. 50 sts
Round 33: K7, k2tog, ssk, k14, k2tog, ssk, k21. 46 sts
Round 34: K6, k2tog, ssk, k12, k2tog, ssk, k20. 42 sts
Round 35: (K2tog, k5) 6 times. 36 sts
Round 36: (K2tog, k4) 6 times. 30 sts
Round 37: (K2tog, k3) 6 times. 24 sts
Bind off, leaving a long tail for seaming.

Tail
Using MC and double pointed needles, CO36, pm, join to knit in the round.
Round 1: K1, ssk, k30, k2tog, k1. 34 sts
Round 2: K1, ssk, k28, k2tog, k1. 32 sts
Round 3: K1, ssk, k26, k2tog, k1. 30 sts
Round 4: Knit.
Round 5: K1, ssk, k24, k2tog, k1. 28 sts
Round 6: Knit.
Round 7: K1, ssk, k22, k2tog, k1. 26 sts
Round 8: Knit.

Round 9: K1, ssk, k20, k2tog, k1. 24 sts
Round 10: Knit.
Round 11: K1, ssk, k18, k2tog, k1. 22 sts
Rounds 12–14: Knit.
Round 15: K1, ssk, k16, k2tog, k1. 20 sts
Rounds 16–18: Knit.
Round 19: K1, ssk, k14, k2tog, k1. 18 sts
Rounds 20–22: Knit.
Round 23: K1, ssk, k12, k2tog, k1. 16 sts
Rounds 24–39: Knit.
Round 40: K1, ssk, k10, k2tog, k1. 12 sts
Round 41: K1, ssk, k8, k2tog, k1. 10 sts
Round 42: K1, ssk, k6, k2tog, k1. 8 sts
Round 43: K1, ssk, k4, k2tog, k1. 6 sts
Break yarn, pull tail through remaining sts, knot, pull knot to inside of toy.

Feet (knit 2)
Using MC and double pointed needles, CO6, pm, join to knit in the round.
Round 1: Kfb 6 times. 12 sts
Round 2: (Kfb, k1) 6 times. 18 sts
Round 3: (Kfb, k2) 6 times. 24 sts
Knit 7 rounds even. Bind off, leaving a 10 in. tail for seaming.

Arms (knit 2)
Using MC and double pointed needles, CO6, pm, join to knit in the round.
Round 1: Kfb 6 times. 12 sts
Round 2: (Kfb, k1) 6 times. 18 sts
Round 3: (Kfb, k2) 6 times. 24 sts
Rounds 4–9: Knit.
Round 10: (K1, ssk, k6, k2tog, k1) twice. 20 sts
Rounds 11–12: Knit.
Round 13: (K1, ssk, k4, k2tog, k1) twice. 16 sts
Knit 6 rounds even. Bind off, leaving a 10 in. tail for seaming.

Spine
Using US size 6 (4.00mm) straight needles and CC yarn, CO2.
Row 1: Knit.
Row 2: Kfb, k1. 3 sts
Row 3: K2, kfb. 4 sts.
Row 4: Kfb, k3. 5 sts.
Row 5: Knit.
Row 6: Ssk, k3. 4 sts.
Row 7: K2, k2tog. 3 sts
Row 8: Ssk, k1. 2 sts
Repeat all 8 rows 12 times.

Assembly

Stuff the head, body, tail, and feet firmly. Stuff the arms lightly. Center the head on the body, and use the tail of the yarn to seam into place, (see figure 1). Seam the feet to the bottom of the body, (see figure 2).

Balancing the body upright on the feet, pin the tail into place, so that the dragon stands up straight. Seam the tail, (see figure 3). Press the arms slightly flat and seam to the sides of the body.

Sew the tail along the center of the back, beginning with the tip of the tail, (see figure 4).

Cut all felt pieces from the template. Sew the eyes to the face, using a coordinating color of thread, (see figure 5). Use a length of black floss to sew on the smile. Sew the teeth onto the edges of the mouth.

For the wings, pair the pieces of light green felt to make two wings of double thickness.

Cut a long length of dark green floss. Use 1 strand of light green floss to whip-stitch the edges together, running a full thickness of dark green floss along edge for contrast, (see figure 6). Using the same long length of dark green floss, sew a running stitch in two lines along the center of the wings, (see figure 7). Sew the wings onto back of dragon, (see figure 8).

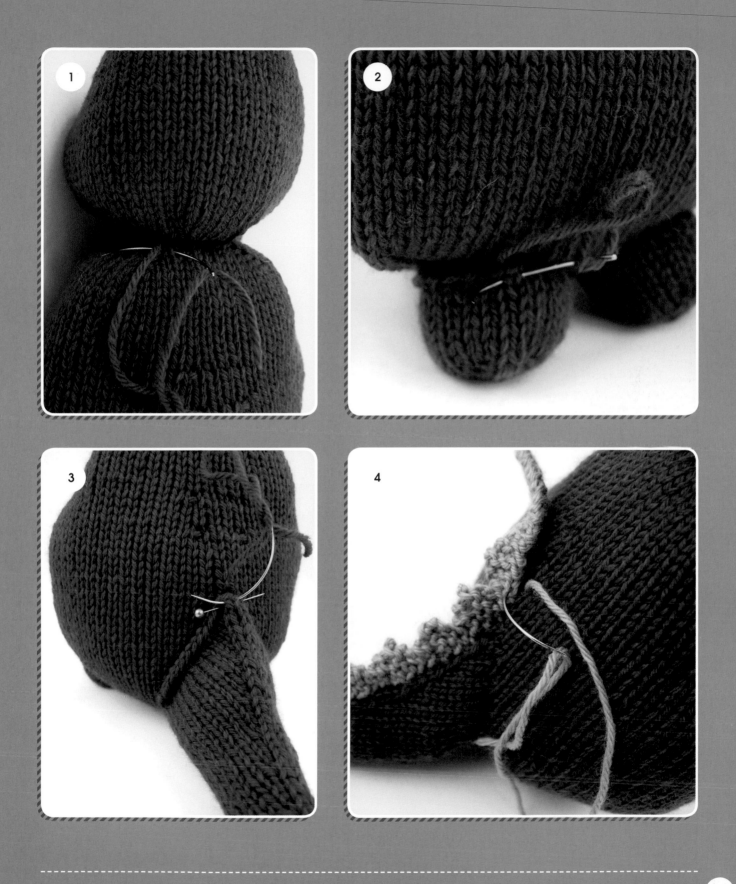

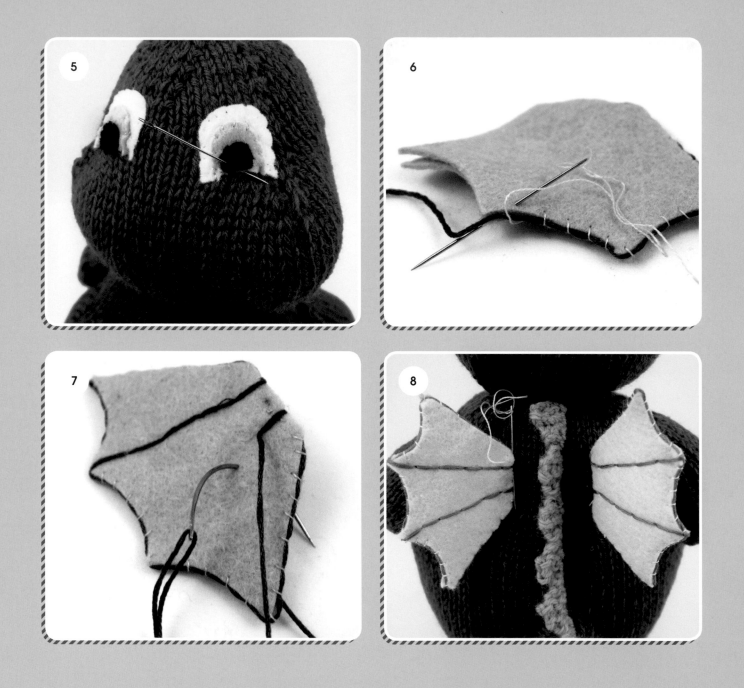

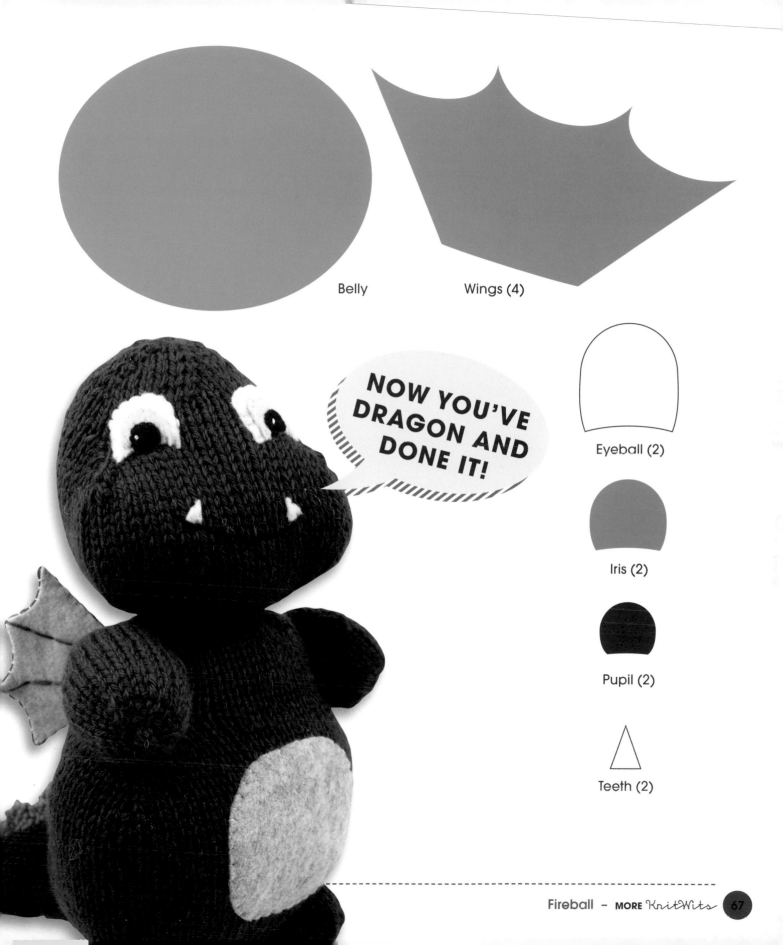

Belly

Wings (4)

NOW YOU'VE DRAGON AND DONE IT!

Eyeball (2)

Iris (2)

Pupil (2)

Teeth (2)

Babushka

There are so many advantages to being nesting monsters. Not only does carrying your children in your mouth make it easier to keep up with them, but it makes many activities much more affordable. The entire Babushka family can go on vacation for the price of one plane ticket. They also pay the admission price for one at movies and amusement parks. The Babushkas practically put the local Chinese buffet out of business, paying for one, but eating for three, or even ten when the extended family comes along. Being a hollow monster means being perpetually hungry.

Materials

- 1 skein Cascade 220 in 2436 (orange)
- 1 skein Cascade 220 in 7804 (pink)
- 1 skein Cascade 220 in 7827 (yellow)
- 1 set US size 6 (4.00mm) double pointed needles
- 1 6-inch plastic egg*
- 1 3-inch plastic egg*
- Sew-on velcro
- Felt in white, blue, green, and black
- Embroidery floss in white, blue, green, orange, pink, and black
- Yarn needle
- Embroidery needle
- Toy stuffing
- Small drill bit

* Plastic eggs come in lots of sizes. The size listed is the height. You can find them year-round online.

Gauge:
20 sts and 26 rows over 4 in. in stockinette st

Finished toy size:
Large monster: 8 in. tall.
Medium monster: 4 in. tall.
Small monster: 2½ in. tall.

Glossary of abbreviations

CO	cast on
k	knit
k2tog	knit two together
kfb	knit into front and back of stitch
p	purl
pm	place marker
ssk	slip, slip, knit slipped stitches together
st[s]	stitch[es]

Weave in loose ends.

Large monster
Top
Using orange yarn, CO66, pm, join to knit in the round.
Rounds 1–6: Knit.
Round 7: (Ssk, k9, k2tog, k9) 3 times. 60 sts
Rounds 8–11: Knit.
Round 12: (Ssk, k8, k2tog, k8) 3 times. 54 sts
Round 13–15: Knit.
Round 16: (Ssk, k7, k2tog, k7) 3 times. 48 sts
Rounds 17–19: Knit.
Round 20: (Ssk, k6, k2tog, k6) 3 times. 42 sts
Rounds 21–23: Knit.

Round 24: (Ssk, k5, k2tog, k5) 3 times. 36 sts
Rounds 25–26: Knit.
Round 27: (Ssk, k4, k2tog, k4) 3 times. 30 sts
Rounds 28–29: Knit.
Round 30: (Ssk, k3, k2tog, k3) 3 times. 24 sts
Rounds 31–32: Knit.
Round 33: (Ssk, k2, k2tog, k2) 3 times. 18 sts
Round 34: Knit.
Round 35: (Ssk, k1, k2tog, k1) 3 times. 12 sts
Round 36: (Ssk, k2tog) 3 times. 6 sts
Break yarn, pull tail through remaining sts, knot, pull knot to inside of fabric.

Bottom
Using orange yarn, CO66, pm, join to knit in the round.
Rounds 1–4: Knit.
Round 5: (Ssk, k9, k2tog, k9) 3 times. 60 sts
Rounds 6–8: Knit.
Round 9: (Ssk, k8, k2tog, k8) 3 times. 54 sts
Round 10–12: Knit.
Round 13: (Ssk, k7, k2tog, k7) 3 times. 48 sts
Rounds 14–15: Knit.
Round 16: (Ssk, k6, k2tog, k6) 3 times. 42 sts
Rounds 17–18: Knit.
Round 19: (Ssk, k5, k2tog, k5) 3 times. 36 sts
Round 20: Knit.
Round 21: (Ssk, k4, k2tog, k4) 3 times. 30 sts
Round 22: Knit.

Round 23: (Ssk, k3, k2tog, k3) 3 times. 24 sts
Round 24: Knit.
Round 25: (Ssk, k2, k2tog, k2) 3 times. 18 sts
Round 26: Knit.
Round 27: (Ssk, k1, k2tog, k1) 3 times. 12 sts
Round 28: (Ssk, k2tog) 3 times. 6 sts
Break yarn, pull tail through remaining sts, knot, pull knot to inside of fabric. Weave in loose ends.

Arms (knit 2)
Using orange yarn, CO6, pm, join to knit in the round.
Round 1: Kfb 6 times. 12 sts
Round 2: (Kfb, k1) 6 times. 18 sts
Knit 12 rounds even.
Round 15: (K2tog, k1) 6 times. 12 sts
Bind off, leaving a 10 in. tail for seaming.

Legs (knit 2)
Using orange yarn, CO6, pm, join to knit in the round.
Round 1: Kfb 6 times. 12 sts
Round 2: (Kfb, k1) 6 times. 18 sts
Round 3: (Kfb, k2) 6 times. 24 sts
Rounds 4–7: Knit.
Round 8: K24, turn.
Begin knitting straight.
Row 9: P2tog, p20, p2tog. 22 sts
Row 10: Ssk, k18, k2tog. 20 sts
Row 11: P2tog, p16, p2tog. 18 sts
Row 12: Ssk, k14, k2tog. 16 sts
Row 13: P2tog, p12, p2tog. 14 sts
Row 14: Ssk, k10, k2tog. 12 sts
Row 15: P2tog, p8, p2tog. 10 sts
Bind off.

Medium monster
Top
Using pink yarn, CO33, pm, join to knit in the round.
Rounds 1–4: Knit.
Round 5: (Ssk, k9) 3 times. 30 sts
Rounds 6–9: Knit.
Round 10: (Ssk, k3, k2tog, k3) 3 times. 24 sts

Rounds 11–13: Knit.
Round 14: (Ssk, k2, k2tog, k2) 3 times. 18 sts
Rounds 15–16: Knit.
Round 17: (Ssk, k1, k2tog, k1) 3 times. 12 sts
Round 18: (Ssk, k2tog) 3 times. 6 sts
Break yarn, pull tail through remaining sts, knot, pull knot to inside of fabric. Weave in loose ends.

Bottom
Using pink yarn, CO33, pm, join to knit in the round.
Rounds 1–4: Knit.
Round 5: (Ssk, k9) 3 times. 30 sts
Rounds 6–8: Knit.
Round 9: (Ssk, k3, k2tog, k3) 3 times. 24 sts
Rounds 10–11: Knit.
Round 12: (Ssk, k2, k2tog, k2) 3 times. 18 sts
Round 13: (Ssk, k1, k2tog, k1) 3 times. 12 sts
Round 14: (Ssk, k2tog) 3 times. 6 sts
Break yarn, pull tail through remaining sts, knot, pull knot to inside of fabric. Weave in loose ends.

Arms (knit 2)
Using pink yarn, CO6, pm, join to knit in the round.
Knit 6 rounds even.
Bind off, leaving a 10 in. tail for seaming.

Legs (knit 2)
Using pink yarn, CO6, pm, join to knit in the round.
Round 1: Kfb 6 times. 12 sts
Round 2: (Kfb, k1) 6 times. 18 sts
Rounds 4–6: Knit.
Round 8: K18, turn.
Begin knitting straight.
Row 9: P2tog, p14, p2tog. 16 sts
Row 10: Ssk, k12, k2tog. 14 sts
Row 11: P2tog, p10, p2tog. 12 sts
Row 12: Ssk, k8, k2tog. 10 sts
Bind off.

Small monster
Using yellow yarn, CO6, pm, join to knit in the round.
Round 1: Knit.
Round 2: Kfb 6 times. 12 sts
Round 3: Knit.
Round 4: (Kfb, k1) 6 times. 18 sts
Rounds 5–6: Knit,
Round 7: (Kfb, k2) 6 times. 24 sts
Rounds 8–10: Knit.
Round 11: (Kfb, k3) 6 times. 30 sts
Rounds 12–15: Knit.
Round 16: (K2tog, k3) 6 times. 24 sts
Round 17: Knit.
Stuff monster.
Round 18: (K2tog, k2) 6 times. 18 sts
Round 19: (K2tog, k1) 6 times. 12 sts
Round 20: K2tog 6 times. 6 sts
Break yarn, pull tail through remaining sts, knot, pull knot to inside of fabric. Weave in loose ends.

Legs (knit 2)
Using yellow yarn, CO6, pm, join to knit in the round.
Knit 4 rounds even. Break yarn, pull tail through remaining sts, knot, pull knot to inside of fabric. Weave in loose ends.

Arms (knit 2)
Using yellow yarn, CO3.
Knit a ½ in. i-cord. Bind off.

Assembly

For each of the plastic egg pieces, use the small drill bit to drill holes every ¼ in. around the perimeter of the opening. Don't worry about sanding the holes. The edge of the hole will help the fabric to stick, (see figure 1). Slide the matching knitted egg piece over the plastic. Using embroidery floss that matches the egg, sew in and out of the holes, securing into place, with the fabric rising just a tiny bit above the plastic edge, (see figure 2). Place the matching egg pieces together, matching decrease rows. Seam together a hinge along the back edge: 2 in. for the large monster, 1 in. for the medium monster, (see figure 3).

Legs
Stuff the legs firmly. Place the legs on the bottom half of each monster, with the diagonal edge running up the side of the body. Seam into place, (see figure 4).

Arms
Do not stuff the arms. Flatten slightly, seam to the upper edge of the monster's bottom half, (see figure 5). For the small monster, sew on i-cord arms 2/3s of the way down the sides of the body.

Cut felt and velcro pieces using template. Sew the soft velcro teeth along the upper edge of the monster bottoms. Matching placement, sew the pricky velcro teeth along upper edge of the monster mouth, (see figure 6).

Center the eyes on the front of the monsters. Sew into place using matching embroidery floss, (see figure 7). Use a full thickness of floss to outline the upper edge of the eye. For the small monster, use black floss to create a smile. Sew the teeth into place along the mouth edge using white thread.

1

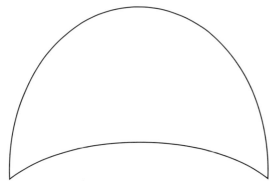

Large monster eyeball

Large monster iris

Large monster pupil

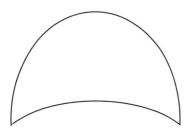

Medium monster eyeball

Medium monster iris

Medium monster pupll

Small monster eyeball

Small monster iris

Small monster pupil

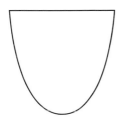

Large monster teeth
Cut 2 from prickly velcro
and 2 from soft velcro

Medium monster teeth
Cut 2 from prickly velcro
and 2 from soft velcro

Small monster teeth
cut from felt

Ada

Ada is a typical little sister, meaning she is really good at getting her big brother into trouble. Ada and her brother quarrel like most siblings. They fight over the TV. They fight over who gets more room in the back seat of the car. They fight over the last cookies in the cupboard, who gets to sit next to mom at the dinner table, whose turn it is to wash dishes, and so on. But Ada has an advantage in these fights. She has the "cute factor". When an argument ensues, her older brother is defiant and mad, but Ada remains calm and smiles sweetly, allowing the blame to consequently fall on her brother. Sometimes, when she's bored, she'll approach her big brother, who is minding his own business, and let out a piercing scream. When her mom comes running, she'll point a finger at her brother and exclaim, "He hit me." While her brother is being dragged off for punishment, Ada just smiles and giggles quietly.

Materials

- 1 skein Cascade 220 Superwash in 878 (MC) beige
- 1 skein Cascade 220 Superwash in 849 (CC1) blue
- 1 skein Cascade 220 Superwash in 815 (CC2) black
- 1 set US size 4 (3.5mm) double pointed needles
- Yarn needle
- Embroidery needle
- Craft felt in black, white, and blue
- Embroidery floss in black, white, and blue
- Toy stuffing
- Two small buttons

Gauge:
24 sts and 32 rows over 4 in. in stockinette st

Finished toy size: 7½ in. tall.

Glossary of abbreviations

CO	cast on
k	knit
k2tog	knit two together
kfb	knit into front and back of stitch
pfb	purl into front and back of stitch
p	purl
pm	place marker
ssk	slip, slip, knit slipped stitches together
st[s]	stitch[es]

Head, knit sideways

Using MC, CO4, pm, join to knit in the round.
Round 1: Kfb 4 times. 8 sts
Round 2: (K1, kfb twice, k1) twice. 12 sts
Round 3: (K1, kfb, k2, kfb, k1) twice. 16 sts
Round 4: Knit.
Round 5: (K1, kfb, k4, kfb, k1) twice. 20 sts
Round 6: Knit.
Round 7: (K1, kfb, k6, kfb, k1) twice. 24 sts
Round 8: Knit.
Round 9: (K1, kfb, k8, kfb, k1) twice. 28 sts
Round 10: Knit.
Round 11: (K1, kfb, k10, kfb, k1) twice. 32 sts
Rounds 12–16: Knit.
Round 17: (K1, ssk, k10, k2tog, k1) twice. 28 sts
Round 18: Knit.
Round 19: (K1, ssk, k8, k2tog, k1) twice. 24 sts
Round 20: Knit.
Round 21: (K1, ssk, k6, k2tog, k1) twice. 20 sts
Round 22: Knit.
Pause and stuff head lightly.
Round 23: (K1, ssk, k4, k2tog, k1) twice. 16 sts
Round 24: (K1, ssk, k2, k2tog, k1) twice. 12 sts
Round 25: (K1, ssk, k2tog, k1) twice. 8 sts
Stuff rest of head lightly.
Round 26: (Ssk, k2tog) twice. 4 sts
Break yarn. Pull tail through remaining sts. Knot, pull tail to inside of head. Press head between hands to get a flat lemon shape.

Body (knit 2)

Front and back, to be joined later.
Begin knitting straight on two double pointed needles Using MC, CO8.
Row 1: Knit.
Row 2 and all even rows: Purl.
Row 3: Knit.
Row 5: K1, kfb, k4, kfb, k1. 10 sts
Row 7: K1, kfb, k6, kfb, k1. 12 sts
Row 9: K1, kfb, k8, kfb, k1. 14 sts
Row 10: Purl. Break yarn. Leave sts on needle.
Once you have both the front and back, reattach MC to one edge. Knit across first 14 sts, then across the 14 sts on the second needle. Pm, join to knit in the round. 28 sts
Arrange stitches on three double pointed needles.

Rounds 1–8: Knit.
Round 9: (K2tog, k2) 7 times. 21 sts
Round 10: Knit.
Round 11: (K2tog, k1) 7 times. 14 sts
Round 12: Knit.
Round 13: K2tog 7 times. 7 sts
Break yarn. Pull tail through remaining sts, knot. Weave in loose end.

Arms (knit 2)

Begin knitting straight on two double pointed needles. Using MC, CO4.
Row 1: Knit.
Row 2 and all even rows: Purl.
Row 3: Knit.
Row 5: K1, kfb twice, k1. 6 sts
Row 7: K1, kfb, k2, kfb, k1. 8 sts
Row 9: K1, kfb, k4, kfb, k1. 10 sts
Divide sts over three double pointed needles, join to knit in the round.
Round 10: Knit.
Round 11: K1, kfb, k6, kfb, k1. 12 sts
Rounds 12–19: Knit.
Round 20: K2tog 6 times. 6 sts
Break yarn. Pull tail through remaining sts, knot. Weave in loose end.

Legs (Knit 2)

Using MC, CO12, pm, join to knit in the round.
Rounds 1–16: Knit.
Round 17: (Kfb, k1) 6 times. 18 sts
Round 18: Knit.
Round 19: (Kfb, k2) 6 times. 24 sts
Rounds 20–21: Knit.
Round 22: (K2tog, k2) 6 times. 18 sts
Round 23: (K2tog, k1) 6 times. 12 sts
Round 24: K2tog 6 times. 6 sts
Break yarn. Pull tail through remaining sts, knot. Weave in loose end.

Dress (knit 2)

Front and back, to be joined later.
Begin knitting straight on two double pointed needles. Using CC1, CO8.
Row 1: Knit.
Row 2 and all even rows: Purl.
Row 3: K1, kfb, k4, kfb, k1. 10 sts
Row 5: K1, kfb, k6, kfb, k1. 12 sts
Row 7: K1, kfb, k8, kfb, k1. 14 sts

Row 9: K1, kfb, k10, kfb, k1. 16 sts
Row 10: Purl. Break yarn. Leave sts on needle.
Once you have both the front and back, reattach CC1 to one edge. Knit across first 16 sts, then across the 16 sts on the second needle. Arrange stitches over three double pointed needles. Pm, join to knit in the round. 32 sts
Rounds 1–10: Knit.
Round 11: (K1, p1) 16 times.
Round 12: (P1, k1) 16 times.
Round 13: (K1, p1) 16 times.
Bind off in the seed stitch pattern.
Weave in loose end.

Shoes (knit 2)

Using CC2, CO5, pm, join to knit in the round.
Round 1: Kfb 5 times. 10 sts
Round 2: (Kfb, k1) 5 times. 15 sts
Round 3: (Kfb, k2) 5 times. 20 sts
Rounds 4–6: Knit.
Round 7: BO8, k12. 12 sts
Turn and begin knitting straight.
Row 8: Purl.
Row 9: Knit.
Row 10: Purl.
Bind off, leaving a long tail to use as shoe strap.

Hair

Using CC2, CO4, pm, join to knit in the round.
Round 1: Kfb 4 times. 8 sts
Round 2: Knit.
Round 3: (K1, kfb twice, k1) twice. 12 sts
Round 4: Knit.
Round 5: (K1, kfb, k2, kfb, k1) twice. 16 sts
Round 6: Knit.
Round 7: (K1, ssk, k2, k2tog, k1) twice. 12 sts
Round 8: (K1, ssk, k2tog, k1) twice. 8 sts
Round 9: (Ssk, k2tog) twice. 4 sts
Round 10: K1, kfb twice, k1. 6 sts
Round 11: K1, kfb, k2, kfb, k1. 8 sts
Turn. Begin knitting straight.
Row 12: P1, pfb twice, p2, pfb, p2. 11 sts
Row 13: K3, kfb, k2, kfb, k2, kfb, k1. 14 sts
Row 14: Purl.

Row 15: K1, ssk, k1, kfb, k2, kfb, k4, kfb, k1. 16 sts
Row 16: Purl.
Row 17: K1, ssk, k1, kfb, k2, kfb, k6, kfb, k1. 18 sts
Row 18: Purl.
Row 19: K1, ssk, k1, kfb, k2, kfb, k10. 19 sts
Row 20: Purl.
Row 21: K1, ssk, k16. 18 sts
Row 22: Purl.
Row 23: Knit.
Row 24: Purl.
Row 25: K1, ssk, k15. 17 sts
Row 26: P14, p2tog, p1. 16 sts
Row 27: K1, ssk, k13K1, ssk, k13. 15 sts. 15 sts
Row 28: P13, pfb, p1. 16 sts
Row 29: K1, kfb, k14. 17 sts
Row 30: P15, pfb, p1. 18 sts
Row 31: K1, kfb, k2tog, k2, ssk, k10. 17 sts
Row 32: P15, pfb, p1. 18 sts
Row 33: K1, kfb, k1, k2tog, k2, ssk, k9. 17 sts
Row 34: Purl.
Row 35: K1, kfb, k1, k2tog, k2, ssk, k8. 16 sts
Row 36: Purl.
Row 37: K1, kfb, k1, k2tog, k2, ssk, k4, k2tog, k1. 14 sts
Row 38: Purl.
Row 39: K1, kfb, k1, k2tog, k2, ssk, k2, k2tog, k1. 12 sts
Row 40: P1, p2tog twice, p2, p2tog twice, p1. 8 sts
Pm, return to knitting in the round.
Round 41: K2, k2tog, ssk, k2. 6 sts
Round 42: K1, k2tog, ssk, k1. 4 sts
Round 43: Kfb 4 times. 8 sts
Round 44: (K1, kfb twice, k1) twice. 12 sts
Round 45: (K1, kfb, k2, kfb, k1) twice. 16 sts
Round 46: Knit.
Round 47: (K1, ssk, k2, k2tog, k1) twice. 12 sts
Round 48: Knit.
Round 49: (K1, ssk, k2tog, k1) twice. 8 sts
Round 50: (Ssk, k2tog) twice. 4 sts
Break yarn. Pull tail through remaining sts, knot, pull to inside of ponytail.

Assembly

Press the arms and body lightly. Line up the arms against the side of the body. Pin in place if needed.

Using MC, seam together, beginning at the upper edge, working under the arm, and back up the other side, (see figure 1). Stuff the body and arms firmly.

Center the head on the top of the body. Seam around edge of the neck, (see figure 2).

Stuff the legs, firmly in the feet, and lightly in the leg. Seam to the underside of the body, (see figure 3).

Pull the dress up over the body. Pull the tails across the shoulders and use as straps. Knot into place, weave in loose ends, (see figure 4).

Pull the shoes tightly over the feet. Pull the tails across as straps, weaving through one side, then back across again. Knot into place, weave in loose ends, (see figure 5).

Press the hair lightly. Place on the head, pinning into place to keep the edge from rolling. Using CC2, sew through the hair layer in a running stitch around the edge, (see figure 6). Tie a strand of CC1 around each ponytail.

Cut felt pieces using the template. Use coordinating thread color to sew the eye into place, (see figure 7). Use a full thickness of black embroidery floss to embroider on eyelashes and a smile. Sew buttons to the front of dress.

1

2

3

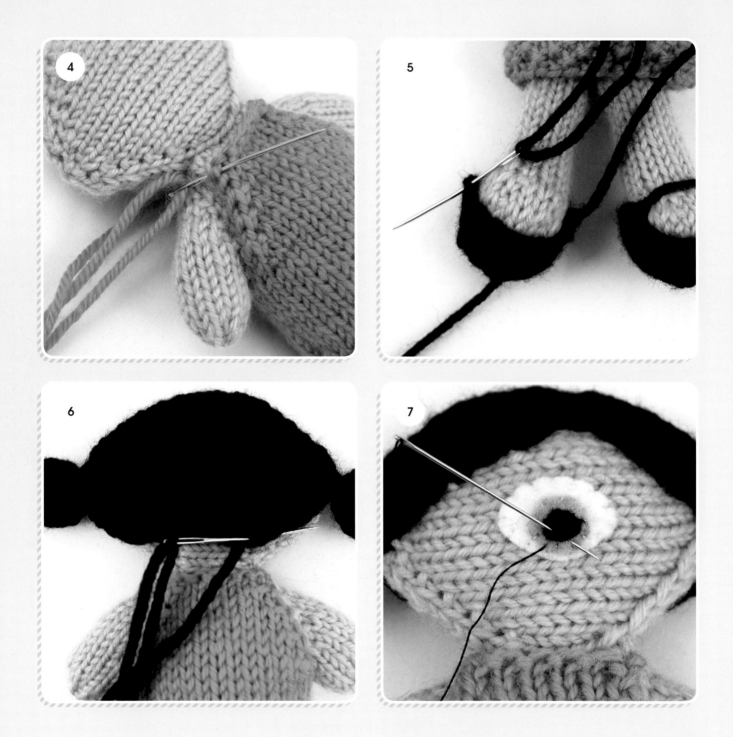

Eyeball

Iris

Pupil

CUTE BUT DEADLY...LIKE A FURRY SHARK!

Rutentuten

Nothing makes Rutentuten grumpier than being awakened from the dead. Every time he gets settled in, all cozy in his sarcophagus deep in the pyramid, those darned archaeologists barge in, making such a racket. Just when he thought he was finally rid of them, they were followed by the worst interruption of all, American tourists. It's no wonder mummies have the reputation of being less than friendly. I'd be pretty curmudgeonly too if someone kept interrupting my 5,000 year nap.

Materials

- 1 skein Cascade 220 in 8555 (black)
- 1 skein Cascade 220 in 8505 (white)
- 1 set US size 6 (4.00mm) double pointed needles
- Toy stuffing
- Yarn needle
- Embroidery needle
- Felt in black and white

Gauge:
20 sts and 26 rows over 4 in. in stockinette st

Finished toy size:
9½ in. tall.

Glossary of abbreviations

CO	cast on
k	knit
k2tog	knit two together
kfb	knit into front and back of stitch
p	purl
pm	place marker
ssk	slip, slip, knit slipped stitches together
st[s]	stitch[es]

Head

Knit from the top down.
Using white yarn, CO6, pm, join to knit in the round.
Round 1: Kfb 6 times. 12 sts
Round 2 and all even numbered rounds: Knit.
Round 3: (Kfb, k1) 6 times. 18 sts
Round 5: (Kfb, k2) 6 times. 24 sts
Round 7: (Kfb, k3) 6 times. 30 sts
Round 9: (Kfb, k4) 6 times. 36 sts
Round 11: (Kfb, k5) 6 times. 42 sts
Round 12: Knit.
Switch to black yarn.
Rounds 13–17: Knit.
Switch to white yarn.
Round 18: Knit.
Round 19: (K2tog, k5) 6 times. 36 sts
Round 21: (K2tog, k4) 6 times. 30 sts
Round 23: (K2tog, k3) 6 times. 24 sts
Bind off.

Body

Knit from the bottom up.
Using white yarn, CO6, pm, join to knit in the round.
Round 1: Kfb 6 times. 12 sts
Round 2 and all even numbered rounds: Knit.
Round 3: (Kfb, k1) 6 times. 18 sts
Round 5: (Kfb, k2) 6 times. 24 sts
Round 7: (Kfb, k3) 6 times. 30 sts
Round 9: (Kfb, k4) 6 times. 36 sts
Round 11: (Kfb, k5) 6 times. 42 sts
Rounds 12–24: Knit.
Round 25: (K2tog, k5) 6 times. 36 sts
Round 27: (K2tog, k4) 6 times. 30 sts
Round 29: (K2tog, k3) 6 times. 24 sts
Bind off.

Legs (knit 2)

Using white yarn, CO6, pm, join to knit in the round.
Round 1: Kfb 6 times. 12 sts
Round 2 and all even numbered rounds: Knit.
Round 3: (Kfb, k1) 6 times. 18 sts
Round 5: (Kfb, k2) 6 times. 24 sts
Rounds 6–8: Knit.
Round 9: (K2tog, k6) 3 times. 21 sts
Rounds 10–12: Knit.
Round 13: (K2tog, k5) 3 times. 18 sts
Rounds 14–24: Knit.
Bind off.

Arms (knit 2)

Using white yarn, CO6, pm, join to knit in the round.
Round 1: Kfb 6 times. 12 sts
Round 2 and all even numbered rounds: Knit.
Round 3: (Kfb, k1) 6 times. 18 sts
Rounds 4–8: Knit.
Round 9: (K2tog, k4) 3 times. 15 sts
Rounds 10–19: Knit.
Bind off.

Assembly

Stuff all pieces firmly. Weave in loose ends.
Cut all felt pieces using template.
Eyes: Center the eyes on the black stripe. Sew into place using white thread for the eyeball and black thread for the pupil, (see figure 1).
When sewing bandages into place, overlap slightly to cover knitted fabric.

Head bandages

Center one A piece on top of the head. Sew into place using white thread, (see figure 2). Wrap a B piece around the edge of the A piece you just attached, keeping the seam on the back of the head. Sew down back seam, around bottom edge, and back up center seam. Leave the top edge free, (see figure 3). Wrap a C piece around the head, lining the bottom edge white top of black stripe, just above eyes. Sew into place, leaving top edge free.

Center another B piece around the bottom of the head. Sew up center seam, around upper edge, and back down center seam. Wrap a D piece around the lower middle of the head, slanting slightly so that the seam meets in the back of the head, covering the black stripe, but leaving the eyes visible in the front. Seam around the bottom edge, leaving the top edge free, (see figure 4).

Body bandages

Center an A piece on the bottom of the body. Sew into place same as for head, (see figure 2). Sew a B piece on the top and bottom edges of body, same as for head, (see figure 3). Wrap a C piece around the bottom edge of the B piece at the top of the body. Sew into place around the bottom edge, leaving the top edge free, (see figure 5). Wrap another C piece around the bottom edge of the first C piece. Sew into place around the bottom edge. Follow with a 3rd C piece, covering the last of the body.

Arm bandages

Wrap a G piece around the wrist. Sew into place around top edge, (see figure 6). Wrap an F piece around the upper edge of the G piece, meeting at the back seam, and then spiraling up until the full arm is covered. Seam into place along the upper edge as you go, (see figure 7).

Leg bandages

Wrap an H piece around the ankle. Sew into place around the top edge, same as for the arms. Wrap an E piece around upper edge of the H piece, meeting at the back seam, and then spiraling up until the full leg is covered. Seam into place along the upper edge as you go, just as for the arms.

Center the head on top of the body, lining up the bandage seams in back. Sew into place using white thread, (see figure 8). Sew the legs to the bottom of the body using white thread. Flatten arms slightly at the upper edge. Pin to the sides of the body at the desired position. Sew into place, (see figure 9).

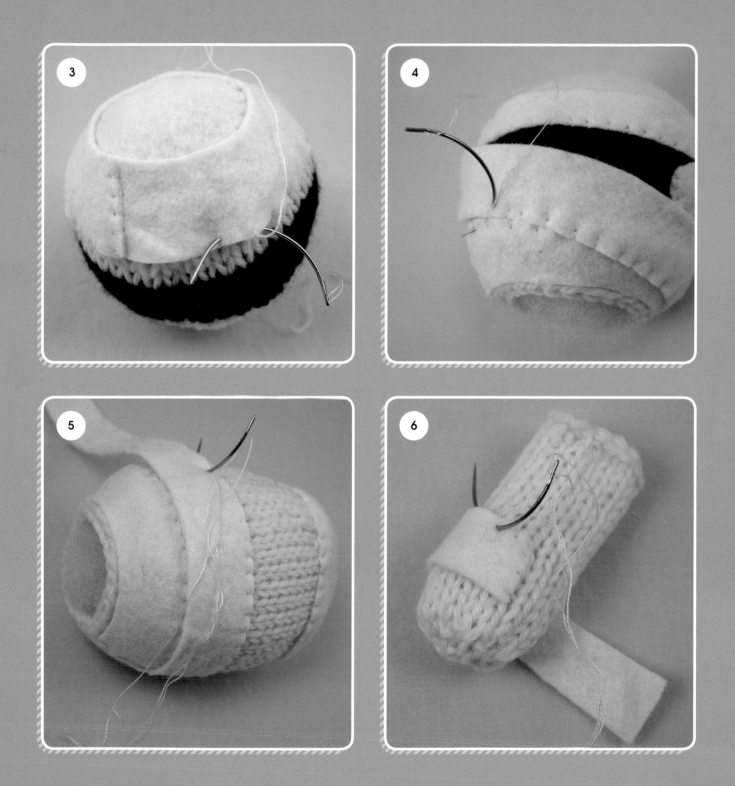

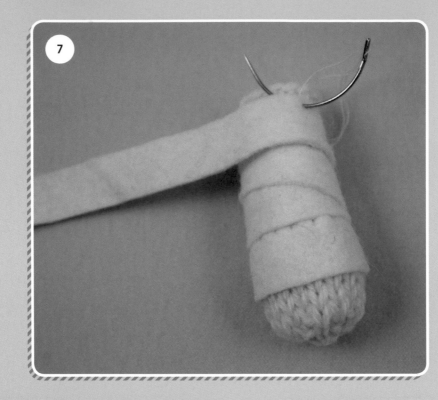

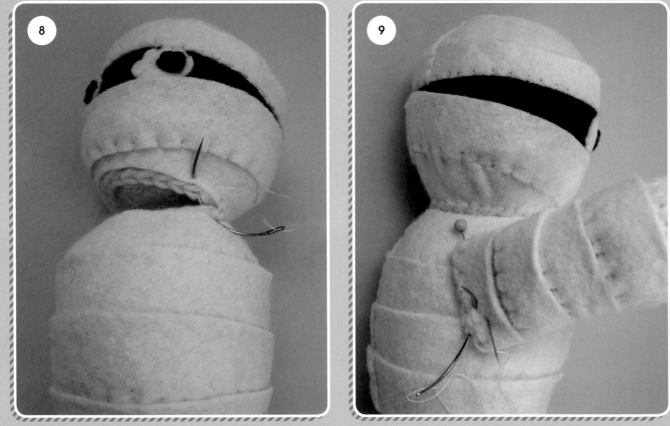

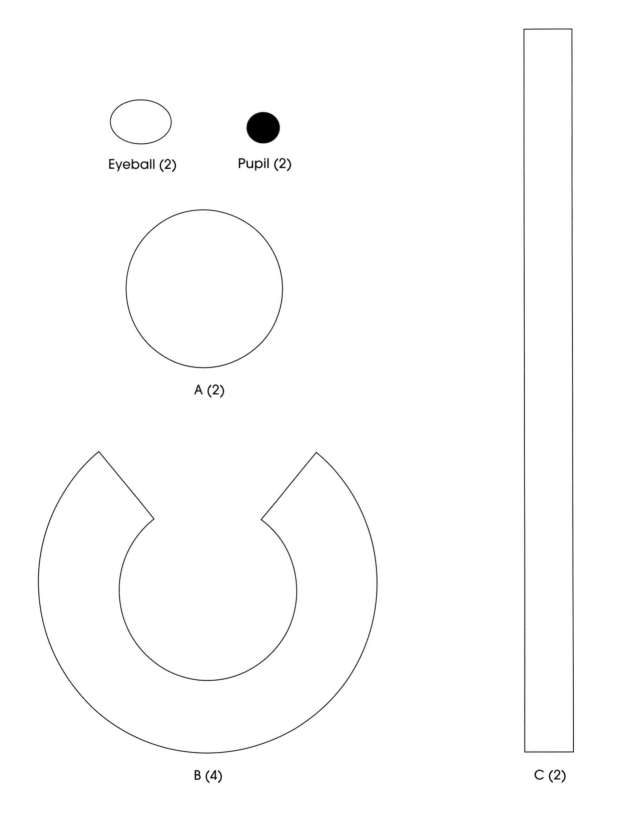

Eyeball (2)

Pupil (2)

A (2)

B (4)

C (2)

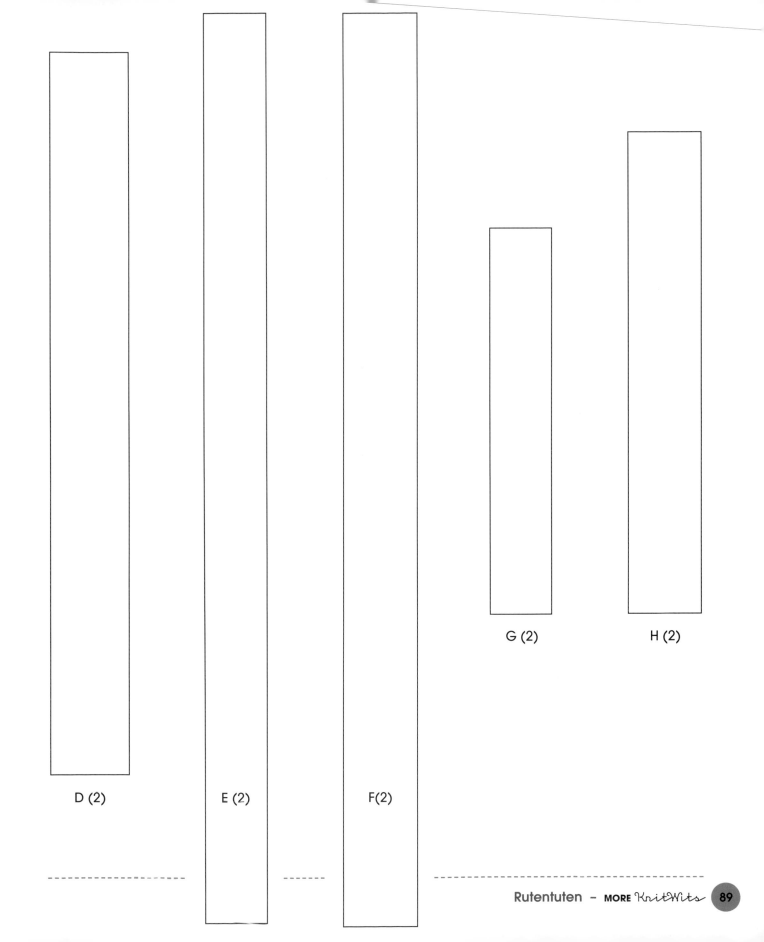

D (2)

E (2)

F(2)

G (2)

H (2)

Brody

When Brody was a young monster, he won a trip to space camp. That magical week transformed him, and all he could dream of was the day he'd become a real astronaut. But when Brody hit adolescence, his horns came in, and along with them came the realization that an astronaut's helmet would never fit on his head. He was devastated. Fast forward 30 years, and Brody is a file clerk at NASA headquarters. He doesn't love his job, but it does pay the bills. He tries to keep in good spirits, but sometimes it's difficult. If you happen to be at headquarters on a shuttle launch day, don't be surprised if you see Brody, pushing his file cart and staring out the window, a tear sliding down his sad green face.

Materials

- 1 skein Cascade 220 in 8903 (MC) green
- 1 skein Cascade 220 in 2411 (CC) brown
- 1 set US size 6 (4.00mm) double pointed needles
- Pieces of wool felt in white, black, and green
- Toy stuffing
- Yarn needle
- Embroidery needle
- Embroidery floss in white, black, and green

Gauge:
20 sts and 26 rows over 4 in. in stockinette st

Finished toy size:
9 in. tall.

Glossary of abbreviations

CO	cast on
k	knit
k2tog	knit two together
kfb	knit into front and back of stitch
pfb	purl into front and back of stitch
p	purl
pm	place marker
ssk	slip, slip, knit slipped stitches together
st[s]	stitch[es]

Body, knit from the top down
Using MC, CO16, pm, join to knit in the round.
Round 1: (K1, kfb, k4, kfb, k1) twice. 20 sts
Round 2: (K1, kfb, k6, kfb, k1) twice. 24 sts
Round 3: (K1, kfb, k8, kfb, k1) twice. 28 sts
Round 4: (K1, kfb, k10, kfb, k1) twice. 32 sts
Round 5: (K1, kfb, k12, kfb, k1) twice. 36 sts
Round 6: (K1, kfb, k14, kfb, k1) twice. 40 sts
Round 7: Knit.
Round 8: (K1, kfb, k16, kfb, k1) twice. 44 sts
Round 9: Knit.
Round 10: (K1, kfb, k18, kfb, k1) twice. 48 sts
Rounds 11–20: Knit.
Round 21: (K1, ssk, k18, k2tog, k1) twice. 44 sts

Rounds 22–24: Knit.
Round 25: (K1, ssk, k16, k2tog, k1) twice. 40 sts
Rounds 26–48: Knit.
Stuff body, pressing flat to push stuffing into edges.

Begin dividing for legs
Knit the first 10 sts on one double pointed needle. Move the next 20 sts to a piece of scrap yarn. Knit the last 10 sts on a second double pointed needle. Continue knitting in the round. 20 sts, (see figure 1).
Rounds 1–7: Knit.
Round 8: (K2tog, k2) 5 times. 15 sts
Round 9: (K2tog, k1) 5 times. 10 sts
Stuff leg.
Round 10: K2tog 5 times. 5 sts
Break yarn, pull tail through remaining sts. Knot, pull knot to inside of foot.
Pick up sts from scrap yarn, dividing between two needles. Reattach MC at edge, pm, begin knitting in the round.
Follow rounds 1–10, same as for first foot.

Arms (knit 2)
Using MC, CO6, pm, join to knit in the round.
Round 1: Kfb 6 times. 12 sts
Rounds 2–4: Knit.
Round 5: Kfb, k11. 13 sts
Rounds 6–7: Knit.
Round 8: Kfb, k12. 14 sts
Rounds 9–10: Knit.
Round 11: Kfb, k13. 15 sts
Rounds 12–16: Knit.
Stuff arm.
Round 17: (K2tog, k1) 5 times. 10 sts
Round 18: K2tog 5 times. 5 sts
Break yarn, pull tail through remaining sts, knot, pull knot to inside of arm.

Horns
Lower horn (knit 2)
Using CC, CO2, begin knitting straight

on double pointed needles.
Row 1: Kfb twice. 4 sts
Row 2: Pfb, p2, pfb. 6 sts
Row 3: Kfb, k4, kfb. 8 sts
Row 4: Pfb, p6, pfb. 10 sts
Divide sts between three needles, pm,
begin knitting in the round.
Rounds 5–10: Knit.
Bind off.

Assembly

Arms
Pin the arms to the side of the body. Use
MC to sew into place, (see figure 2).

Horns
Stuff the upper horns. Connect the
lower horn to upper, so that the diagonal
edges form a right angle. Sew together
using CC, (see figure 3). Stuff the lower
horn. Pin the horns to the side of the
head. Sew into place, (see figure 4).

Cut felt pieces using the template. Place
the eyes on the head. Sew into place,
using corresponding color of thread,
(see figure 5). Use a full thickness of
black embroidery floss to outline the
eyes and to create a down-turned mouth,
(see figure 6). Place the teeth at the
edges of the mouth. Use white thread to
sew into place, (see figure 7).

Upper horn (knit 2)
Using CC, CO2, begin knitting straight
on double pointed needles.
Row 1: Kfb twice. 4 sts
Row 2: Pfb, p2, pfb. 6 sts
Row 3: Kfb, k4, kfb. 8 sts
Row 4: Pfb, p6, pfb. 10 sts
Divide sts between three needles, pm,
begin knitting in the round.

Rounds 5–8: Knit.
Round 9: K2tog, k6, k2tog. 8 sts
Rounds 10–12: Knit.
Round 13: K2tog, k4, k2tog. 6 sts
Rounds 14–16: Knit.
Round 17: K2tog, k2, k2tog. 4 sts
Break yarn, pull tail through remaining sts,
knot, pull knot to inside of horn.

1

Eyeball (2)

Eyelid (2)

Pupil (2)

Teeth (2)

Pablo

Pablo always wanted to be a cowboy. This is an unusual aspiration for a bull. He met with a lot of obstacles. First of all, the other cowboys had a serious prejudice against bulls in general. Then there's the problem of finding a cowboy hat that would fit over his horns. And lastly, Pablo looked everywhere, but could not find a horse that was willing to give him a ride. Perhaps you are saying to yourself, "A bull riding a horse? How absurd!" But Pablo is stubborn. He's the reason they coined the term "bull-headed." So while you won't see him in your local rodeo anytime soon, don't be surprised if one day you do.

Materials

- 1 skein Cascade 220 in 9497 (MC)
- 1 skein Cascade 220 in 8414 (CC1)
- 1 skein Cascade 220 in 8505 (CC2)
- 1 set US size 6 (4.00mm) double pointed needles
- Pieces of wool felt in white, black, and brown
- Toy stuffing
- Yarn needle
- Embroidery needle
- Embroidery floss in white and black
- Safety pins

Gauge:
20 sts and 26 rows over 4" in stockinette st

Finished toy size:
10" tall.

Glossary of abbreviations

CO	cast on
k	knit
k2tog	knit two together
kfb	knit into front and back of stitch
pm	place marker
ssk	slip, slip, knit slipped stitches together
st[s]	stitch[es]

A note about knitting stripes in the round

When knitting stripes in the round, there will be a step where the colors change. To prevent this, you may choose to use a jogless join:

On color change rounds, change colors by knitting the first stitch of the new color as you usually would. Then, knit the rest of the stitches to the end of the round.

On the next round, slip the first stitch of the new color, then knit the rest of the stitches. On every following round, knit every stitch as usual.

Body

Knit from the top down.

Using CC1 and double pointed needles, CO28, pm, join to knit in the round.
Round 1: (K1, kfb, k10, kfb, k1) twice.
32 sts
Round 2: (K1, kfb, k12, kfb, k1) twice.
36 sts
Round 3: (K1, kfb, k14, kfb, k1) twice.
40 sts
Round 4: (K1, kfb, k16, kfb, k1) twice.
44 sts
Round 5: (K1, kfb, k18, kfb, k1) twice.
48 sts
Round 6: (K1, kfb, k20, kfb, k1) twice.
52 sts
Switch to CC2, running CC1 along the inside, twisting the sts between each row.
Round 7: (K1, kfb, k22, kfb, k1) twice.
56 sts
Round 8: (K1, kfb, k24, kfb, k1) twice.
60 sts
Round 9: (K1, kfb, k26, kfb, k1) twice.
64 sts
Round 10: (K1, kfb, k28, kfb, k1) twice.
68 sts
Rounds 11–12: Knit.
Switch back to CC1.
Rounds 13–18: Knit.
Switch back to CC2.
Rounds 19–21: Knit.
Begin dividing sts for arms. Break yarn.
Place the first 8 sts on a safety pin. Place the next 18 sts on one double pointed needle. Move the next 8 sts to a 2nd safety pin, and the following 8 sts to a 3rd safety pin. Place the next 18 sts on a 2nd double pointed needle.
Place the remaining 8 sts on a 4th safety pin. Reattach CC2 to the edge of the first double pointed needle to begin body, (see figure 1):
Round 1: K18, CO6 onto another needle, k18 from the back needle, CO6 onto a 4th needle.
Pm, join to knit in the round. 48 sts
Round 2: (K1, ssk, k12, k2tog, k7) twice.
44 sts
Round 3: Knit.
Break CC2. Switch to CC1.
Round 4: (K1, ssk, k10, k2tog, k7) twice.
40 sts
Round 5: Knit.
Round 6: (K1, ssk, k8, k2tog, k7) twice.
36 sts
Switch to MC.
Round 7: Knit.

Round 8: (K1, kfb, k8, kfb, k7) twice. 40 sts
Rounds 9–11: Knit.
Round 12: (K1, kfb, k10, kfb, k7) twice. 44 sts
Rounds 13–15: Knit.

Begin dividing for legs:
Place the first 8 sts on a double pointed needle. Move the next 22 sts to a piece of scrap yarn. Place the next 8 sts on a 2nd double pointed needle, and the remaining 6 sts on a 3rd double pointed needle. Begin as follows:
Round 1: K1, kfb, k3, k2tog, k1, CO6 sts to another double pointed needle for inside of leg, k1, ssk, k3, kfb, k7. 28 sts, (see figure 2).
Round 2–4: Knit.
Round 5: K1, kfb, k3, k2tog, k8, ssk, k3, kfb, k7.
Complete rounds 2–5 twice more.
Rounds 14–15: Knit.
Round 16: K1, ssk, k2, k2tog, k8, ssk, k2, k2tog, k7. 24 sts
Round 17: (K2tog, k2) 6 times. 18 sts
Round 18: (K2tog, k1) 6 times. 12 sts
Round 19: K2tog 6 times. 6 sts
Break yarn, pull tail through remaining sts, knot, pull tail into leg.
Place the sts from the scrap yarn onto 3 double pointed needles, splitting as follows: 8 sts on first needle, 6 sts on 2nd needle, 8 sts on 3rd needle. Reattach MC yarn to edge of 3rd needle to begin knitting the 2nd leg as follows:
Round 1: K1, kfb, k3, k2tog, k1, CO6 sts to another double pointed needle for inside of leg, k1, ssk, k3, kfb, k7. 28 sts
Complete same as for first leg, from round 2.

Arms
Place sts from safety pin onto 2 double pointed needles. Attach CC2 to inside edge.
Round 1: K16, CO6 sts onto 3rd needle, pm, join to knit in the round. 22 sts, (see figure 3).
Rounds 2–3: Knit.
Break CC2, switch to MC.
Rounds 4–14: Knit.

Round 15: Ssk, k12, k2tog, k6. 20 sts
Round 16: (K2tog, k2) 5 times. 15 sts
Round 17: (K2tog, k1) 5 times. 10 sts
Round 18: K2tog 5 times. 5 sts
Break yarn, pull tail through remaining sts, knot, pull to inside of arm.
Pick up sts from other arm and complete same as for first arm.

Head
Using MC and double pointed needles, CO22, pm, join to knit in the round.
Round 1: (K1, kfb, k7, kfb, k1) twice. 26 sts
Round 2: (K1, kfb, k9, kfb, k1) twice. 30 sts
Round 3: (K1, kfb, k11, kfb, k1) twice. 34 sts
Round 4: (K1, kfb, k13, kfb, k1) twice. 38 sts
Round 5: (K1, kfb, k15, kfb, k1) twice. 42 sts
Rounds 6–10: Knit.
Round 11: (K1, ssk, k15, k2tog, k1) twice. 38 sts
Round 12 and all remaining even rounds: Knit.
Round 13: (K1, ssk, k13, k2tog, k1) twice. 34 sts
Round 15: (K1, ssk, k11, k2tog, k1) twice. 30 sts
Round 17: (K1, ssk, k9, k2tog, k1) twice. 26 sts
Round 19: (K1, ssk, k7, k2tog, k1) twice. 22 sts
Round 21: (K1, ssk, k5, k2tog, k1) twice. 18 sts
Round 23: (K1, ssk, k3, k2tog, k1) twice. 14 sts
Round 25: (K1, ssk, k1, k2tog, k1) twice. 10 sts
Round 27: K2tog 5 times.
Break yarn, pull tail through remaining sts, knot, pull to inside of head.

Horns (knit 2)
Using CC2, CO12, pm, join to knit in the round.
Round 1: Knit.
Round 2: Ssk, k3, kfb twice, k3, k2tog.

Round 3: Knit.
Round 4: Ssk, k3, kfb twice, k3, k2tog.
Round 5: Knit.
Round 6: Ssk, k3, kfb twice, k3, k2tog.
Rounds 7–9: Knit.
Round 10: Kfb, k3, k2tog, ssk, k3, kfb.
Round 11: K4, k2tog, ssk, k4. 10 sts
Round 12: Kfb, k2, k2tog, ssk, k2, kfb.
Round 13: K3, k2tog, ssk, k3. 8 sts
Round 14: Kfb, k1, k2tog, ssk, k1, kfb.
Round 15: K2, k2tog, ssk, k2. 6 sts
Round 16: Kfb, k2tog, ssk, kfb.
Round 17: K1, k2tog, ssk, k1. 4 sts
Break yarn, pull tail through remaining sts, knot, pull to inside of horn.
Round 1: Kfb 6 times. 12 sts
Round 2 and all even numbered rounds: Knit.
Round 3: (Kfb, k1) 6 times. 18 sts
Rounds 4–8: Knit.
Round 9: (K2tog, k4) 3 times. 15 sts
Rounds 10–19: Knit.
Bind off.

Assembly

Stuff the body, pushing stuffing firmly into legs and arms. Seam opening closed, (see figure 4).
Stuff the head, seam the top closed.
Seam the horns to the sides of the head, (see figure 5).
Cut felt pieces using the template. Sew the eyes to the face using a coordinating color of floss, (see figure 6).
Center the head at top of the body. Pin into place if needed. Sew into place from underneath, (see figure 7).

Right eyebrow   Left eyebrow

Right eyeball   Left eyeball

Iris (2)

Pupil (2)

IT'S A
COWBOY AND
BULL STORY!

Clink

Clink was built as a spy-bot. He has an indestructible alloy body, X-ray vision, wireless capabilities, and his antenna doubles as a poisonous dart gun. I would love to tell you about all of Clink's top secret assignments, but then I'd have to kill you. I'd also love to tell you that he has been successful at all his espionage, but I can't. You see, Clink has one fatal flaw. He's very noisy. When his creators were building him, they neglected to consider the fact that an indestructible metal body sounds much like a tank coming down the street. So Clink was forced into early retirement. He now resides in the Pacific Northwest, where he raises homing pigeons, and whale watches on the weekends.

Materials

- 1 skein Cascade 220 in 2442
- Small amount of black yarn
- 1 set US size 5 (3.75mm) double pointed needles
- 1 pair US size 5 (3.75mm) straight needles
- Yarn needle
- Embroidery needle
- Felt in blue, black, and white
- Thread in blue, black, and white
- Toy stuffing

Gauge:
20 sts and 28 rows over 4 in. in stockinette st

Finished toy size:
11 in. tall.

Glossary of abbreviations

CO	cast on
k	knit
k2tog	knit two together
kfb	knit into front and back of stitch
pfb	purl into front and back of stitch
p	purl
pm	place marker
ssk	slip, slip, knit slipped stitches together
st[s]	stitch[es]

Head

Top and bottom (knit 2)
Using straight needles, CO7.
Row 1: K1, kfb, k3, kfb, k1. 9 sts
Row 2: P1, pfb, p5, pfb, p1. 11 sts
Row 3: K1, kfb, k7, kfb, k1. 13 sts
Row 4: P1, pfb, p9, pfb, p1. 15 sts
Row 5: K1, kfb, k11, kfb, k1. 17 sts
Row 6: Purl.
Row 7: K1, kfb, k13, kfb, k1. 19 sts
Row 8: Purl.
Row 9: K1, kfb, k15, kfb, k1. 21 sts
Rows 10–14: Work in stockinette st.
Row 15: K1, ssk, k15, k2tog, k1. 19 sts
Row 16: Purl.
Row 17: K1, ssk, k13, k2tog, k1. 17 sts
Row 18: Purl.
Row 19: K1, ssk, k11, k2tog, k1. 15 sts
Row 20: P1, p2tog, p9, p2tog, p1. 13 sts
Row 21: K1, ssk, k7, k2tog, k1. 11 sts
Row 22: P1, p2tog, p5, p2tog, p1. 9 sts
Row 23: K1, ssk, k3, k2tog, k1. 7 sts
Bind off.

Center of head
Using double pointed needles, CO55, pm, join to knit in the round.
Knit 19 rows even. Bind off.

Body

Using double pointed needles, CO35, pm, join to knit in the round.
Knit 16 rows even. Bind off.

Bottom of body
Using straight needles, CO5.
Row 1: K1, kfb, k1, kfb, k1. 7 sts
Row 2: P1, pfb, p3, pfb, p1. 9 sts
Row 3: K1, kfb, k5, kfb, k1. 11 sts
Row 4: Purl.
Row 5: K1, kfb, k7, kfb, k1. 13 sts
Row 6: Purl.
Row 7: K1, kfb, k9, kfb, k1. 15 sts
Rows 8–10: Work in stockinette st.
Row 11: K1, ssk, k9, k2tog, k1. 13 sts
Row 12: Purl.
Row 13: K1, ssk, k7, k2tog, k1. 11 sts
Row 14: Purl.
Row 15: K1, ssk, k5, k2tog, k1. 9 sts
Row 16: P1, p2tog, p3, p2tog, p1. 7 sts
Row 17: K1, ssk, k1, k2tog, k1. 5 sts
Bind off.

Legs (knit 2)

Using double pointed needles, CO5, pm, join to knit in the round.
Round 1: Kfb 5 times. 10 sts
Round 2: (Kfb, k1) 5 times. 15 sts
Round 3: (Kfb, k2) 5 times. 20 sts
Rounds 4–6: Knit.
Round 7: (K2tog, k2) 5 times. 15 sts
Rounds 8–28: Knit.
Bind off.

Arms (knit 2)

Using double pointed needles, CO6, pm, join to knit in the round.
Round 1: Kfb 6 times. 12 sts
Rounds 2–4: Knit.

Round 5: Kfb, k11. 13 sts
Rounds 6–8: Knit.
Round 9: Kfb, k12. 14 sts
Rounds 10–12: Knit.
Round 13: Kfb, k13. 15 sts
Rounds 14–16: Knit.
Stuff arm lightly.
Round 17: (K2tog, k1) 5 times. 10 sts
Round 18: K2tog 5 times. 5 sts
Break yarn, pull tail through remaining sts, knot, and pull knot to inside of arm.

Antenna

Using double pointed needles and black yarn, CO3. Knit a 1 ½ in. i-cord.
Bind off.

Assembly

Head and body

Press all flat pieces lightly. Seam top of head to center of head, around the circumference to make a cylinder. Stuff firmly, pressing stuffing into a round shape. Center bottom of head on cylinder, seam around edge, (see figure 1). Sew bottom of body to body. Stuff firmly. Center head on top of body, and seam into place, (see figure 2).
Stuff legs. Seam to bottom of body, pinning into place if needed. Sew arms to sides of body, (see figure 3).
For seam detail, line seam lines of body with black yarn. Use black thread to hold in place if needed. Use black thread to create a center seam on body and head, (see figure 4).
Use black thread to create knots in a row for the rivets.

Eyes

Cut eyes using felt templates. Sew onto face using corresponding color, (see figure 5).

Antenna

Sew antenna to top of head using tail, (see figure 6).

4

5

6

I ONLY KNOW ONE DANCE!

Eyeball (2)

Iris (2)

Pupil (2)

Joe and Cornelius

This is the classic tale of the bully and the bullied. Cornelius was the smallest kid in his class. He was teased and picked on, never invited to birthday parties, and in his teenage years, was reduced to taking his sister as his prom date. Despite the humiliations of his adolescence, he grew up to be clever and successful. Joe on the other hand was hindered by his intimidating size and lack of social skills. He made up for this by excelling at athletics, and intimidating the little guys. But once his glory days on the water polo court were over, he was forced to take a low paying job, as Cornelius's limo driver.

Materials

- 1 skein Cascade 220 in 9473
- 1 set US size 6 (4.00mm) double pointed needles
- Small scrap of worsted weight yarn for little fish (I used Cascade 220 in 2436)
- Craft felt in white, black, and blue
- Embroidery floss in black and white
- Yarn needle
- Embroidery needle
- Toy stuffing
- Small pieces of thin cardboard (optional)

Gauge:
20 sts and 26 rows over 4 in. in stockinette st

Finished toy size:
Joe : 12 in. long.
Cornelius: 2½ in. long.

Glossary of abbreviations

CO	cast on
k	knit
k2tog	knit two together
kfb	knit into front and back of stitch
p	purl
pm	place marker
ssk	slip, slip, knit slipped stitches together
st[s]	stitch[es]

Joe

Lower jaw

Using MC and double pointed needles, CO14, pm, join to knit in the round.
Round 1: (K1, kfb, k3, kfb, k1) twice. 18 sts
Round 2: (K1, kfb, k5, kfb, k1) twice. 22 sts
Round 3: (K1, kfb, k7, kfb, k1) twice. 26 sts
Round 4: (K1, kfb, k9, kfb, k1) twice. 30 sts
Round 5: (K1, kfb, k11, kfb, k1) twice. 34 sts
Round 6: (K1, kfb, k13, kfb, k1) twice. 38 sts
Round 7: K1, kfb, k15, kfb, k7, bo7, k6. 33 sts
Round 8: Knit to end of round.
Row 9: Turn work to begin knitting flat, p33.
Row 10: k7, kfb, k17, kfb, k7. 35 sts
Row 11 and all remaining odd rows: Purl.
Row 12: K1, k2tog, k4, kfb, k19, kfb, k4, ssk, k1.
Row 14: K1, k2tog, k3, kfb, k21, kfb, k3, ssk, k1.
Row 16: K1, k2tog, k30, ssk, k1. 33 sts

Row 18: k1, k2tog, k28, ssk, k1. 31 sts
Row 20: K1, k2tog, k26, ssk, k1. 29 sts
Break yarn. Leave sts on one double pointed needle.

Upper jaw

Using MC and US6 double pointed needles, CO14, pm, join to knit in the round.
Round 1: (K1, kfb, k3, kfb, k1) twice. 18 sts
Round 2: (K1, kfb, k5, kfb, k1) twice. 22 sts
Round 3: (K1, kfb, k7, kfb, k1) twice. 26 sts
Round 4: (K1, kfb, k9, kfb, k1) twice. 30 sts
Round 5: (K1, kfb, k11, kfb, k1) twice. 34 sts
Round 6: (K1, kfb, k13, kfb, k1) twice. 38 sts
Round 7: Knit.
Round 8: K1, kfb, k15, kfb, k7, bo7, k6. 33 sts
Round 9: Knit to end of round.
Row 10: Turn work to begin knitting flat, p33.
Row 11: K7, kfb, k17, kfb, k7. 35 sts

Row 12 and all remaining even rows: Purl.
Row 13: K7, kfb, k7, kfb, k3, kfb, k7, kfb, k7. 39 sts
Row 15: K1, k2tog, k4, kfb, k24, kfb, k4, ssk, k1.
Row 17: K1, k2tog, k14, kfb, k3, kfb, k14, ssk, k1.
Row 19: K1, k2tog, k33, ssk, k1. 37 sts
Row 21: K1, k2tog, k13, kfb, k3, kfb, k13, ssk, k1.
Row 23: K1, k2tog, k31, ssk, k1. 35 sts
Row 25: K1, k2tog, k12, kfb, k3, kfb, k12, ssk, k1.

Break yarn. Leave sts on one double pointed needle.

Connect jaws to begin body
Seam cast on edges of jaws closed, (see figure 1). Place jaws with inside edges together.
Reconnect yarn to inside left edge of lower jaw so that you will begin knitting across top jaw first, (see figure 2). Pm, and begin knitting in the round. Knit 2 rounds even. Pause knitting to line the

insides of the jaw.

Cut jaw pieces from felt using templates. If desired, trace jaw templates onto thin cardboard and cut out for added stability. Insert felt into corresponding jaw, letting the lip overlap the felt, and sew into place, (see figure 3). Close mouth, so that back edges of felt hang out of the back of the head. Sew together using whip stitch, (see figure 4). Insert cardboard pieces into jaw. No need to secure, the stuffing you add later will hold them in place.

Continue knitting

Rounds 1–2: Knit. 64 sts

Round 3: K1, k2tog, k13, kfb, k1, kfb, k13, ssk, k2, k2tog, k10, kfb, k1, kfb, k10, ssk, k1. 64 sts

Round 4 and all even rounds: Knit.

Round 5: K1, k2tog, k29, ssk, k2, k2tog, k21, ssk, k1. 60 sts

Round 7: K1, k2tog, k12, kfb, k1, kfb, k12, ssk, k2, k2tog, k9, kfb, k1, kfb, k9, ssk, k1.

Round 9: K1, k2tog, k27, ssk, k2, k2tog, k17, ssk, k1. 56 sts

Round 11: K1, k2tog, k11, kfb, k1, kfb, k11, ssk, k2, k2tog, k8, kfb, k1, kfb, k8, ssk, k1.

Round 13: K1, k2tog, k25, ssk, k2, k2tog, k15, ssk, k1. 52 sts

Round 15: K1, k2tog, k10, kfb, k1, kfb, k10, ssk, k2, k2tog, k7, kfb, k1, kfb, k7, ssk, k1.

Round 17: K1, k2tog, k10, kfb, k1, kfb, k10, ssk, k2, k2tog, k15, ssk, k1. 50 sts

Round 19: K1, k2tog, k10, kfb, k1, kfb, k10, ssk, k2, k2tog, k13, ssk, k1. 48 sts

Round 21: K1, k2tog, k10, kfb, k1, kfb, k10, ssk, k2, k2tog, k11, ssk, k1. 46 sts

Rounds 22–26: Knit.

Round 27: K1, k2tog, k10, ssk, k1, k2tog, k10, ssk, k16. 42 sts

Round 29: K11, ssk, k1, k2tog, k26. 40 sts

Round 31: K1, k2tog, k7, ssk, k1, k2tog, k7, ssk, k16. 36 sts

Rounds 36–38: Knit.

Pause to stuff body mostly full. Stuff mouth firmly, squeezing into desired shape.

Round 39: K1, k2tog, k15, ssk, k2,
k2tog, k9, ssk, k1. 32 sts

Rounds 40–42: Knit.

Round 43: K1, k2tog, k13, ssk, k2, k2tog, k7, ssk, k1. 28 sts

Rounds 44–46: Knit.

Round 47: K1, k2tog, k11, ssk, k2, k2tog, k5, ssk, k1. 24 sts

Rounds 48–50: Knit.

Stuff rest of body.

Begin tail

Round 51: K4, kfb, k2, kfb, k8, kfb, k2, kfb, k4. 28 sts

Round 52: K5, kfb, k2, kfb, k10, kfb, k2, kfb, k5. 32 sts

Round 53: K6, kfb, k2, kfb, k12, kfb, k2, kfb, k6. 36 sts

Round 54: K7, kfb, k2, kfb, k14, kfb, k2, kfb, k7. 40 sts

Round 55: K8, kfb, k2, kfb, k16, kfb, k2, kfb, k8. 44 sts

Round 56: K9, kfb, k2, kfb, k18, kfb, k2, kfb, k9. 48 sts

Round 57: K10, kfb, k2, kfb, 20, kfb, k2, kfb, k10. 52 sts

Split tail for fins, (see figure 5).

Split the tail between 4 double pointed needles, 13 on each needle. Begin knitting the top fin as follows:

Round 1: K1, k2tog, k8, kfb, k2, kfb, k8, ssk, k1. 26 sts Bring yarn through middle of tail to begin knitting second round of top fin.

Round 2: K1, k2tog, k20, ssk, k1. 24 sts

Round 3: K1, k2tog, k7, kfb, k2, kfb, k7, ssk, k1.

Round 4: K1, k2tog, k18, ssk, k1. 22 sts

Round 5: K1, k2tog, k6, kfb, k2, kfb, k6, ssk, k1.

Round 6: K1, k2tog, k16, ssk, k1. 20 sts

Round 7: K1, k2tog, k14, ssk, k1. 18 sts

Round 8: K1, k2tog, k12, ssk, k1. 16 sts

Round 9: K1, k2tog, k10, ssk, k1. 14 sts

Round 10: K1, k2tog, k8, ssk, k1. 12 sts

Round 11: K1, k2tog, k6, ssk, k1. 10 sts

Round 12: K1, k2tog, k4, ssk, k1. 8 sts

Round 13: K1, k2tog, k2, ssk, k1. 6 sts

Break yarn, draw tail through remaining sts, knot, pull to inside of tail.

Reattach yarn for bottom fin, following directions same as for top fin.

Dorsal fin

Using double pointed needles, CO24, pm, join to knit in the round.

Round 1: Knit.

Round 2: K1, k2tog, k18, ssk, k1. 22 sts

Round 3: K1, k2tog, k16, ssk, k1. 20 sts

Round 4: K1, k2tog, k14, ssk, k1. 18 sts

Continue in this manner, decreasing one stitch at the beginning and end of each round until 6 sts remain. Break yarn, draw tail through remaining sts, knot, pull to inside of fin.

Pectoral fin (knit 2)

Using double pointed needles, CO24, pm, join to knit in the round.

Round 1: Knit.

Round 2: (K1, k2tog, k6, ssk, k1) twice. 20 sts

Round 3 and all odd rounds: Knit.

Round 4: (K1, k2tog, k4, ssk, k1) twice. 16 sts

Round 6: (K1, k2tog, k2, ssk, k1) twice. 12 sts

Round 8: (K1, k2tog, ssk, k1) twice. 8 sts

Round 10: (K1, k2tog, k1) twice. 6 sts

Break yarn, draw tail through remaining sts, knot, pull to inside of fin.

Assemble Joe

Center the dorsal fin at the highest point of the shark body, sew into place. Center the pectoral fins at the sides. Sew into place.

Cut teeth and eyes out of felt using templates. Line the teeth along the inside edge of the mouth, using the border between the knitted fabric and the felt as a guide. Sew into place using white embroidery floss, (see figure 6). Sew the eyes into place on the sides of the head using matching thread, (see figure 7).

Cornelius

Using desired fish color and double pointed needles, CO6, pm, joint to knit in the round:

Round 1: (K1, kfb, k1) twice. 8 sts
Round 2: (K1, kfb twice, k1) twice. 12 sts
Round 3: (K1, kfb, k2, kfb, k1) twice. 16 sts
Rounds 4–6: Knit.

Round 7: (K1, k2tog, k2, ssk, k1) twice. 12 sts
Round 8: Knit.
Round 9: (K1, k2tog, ssk, k1) twice. 8 sts
Round 10–11: Knit.

Fins

Place 4 sts from the top of the fish (2 from the front, 2 from the back) on one double pointed needle. Knit two rounds as an i-cord. Break yarn, pull tail through remaining sts, knot, pull to inside of toy. Place last 4 sts on one needle, complete as for top fin.

Sew the eyes onto the sides of head.
Feed tiny fish to Joe, if desired.

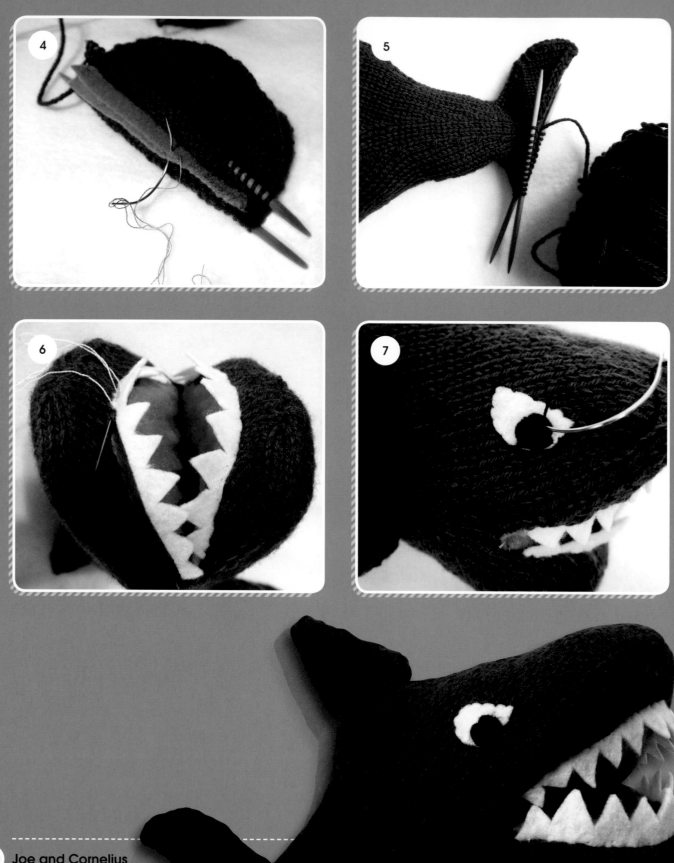

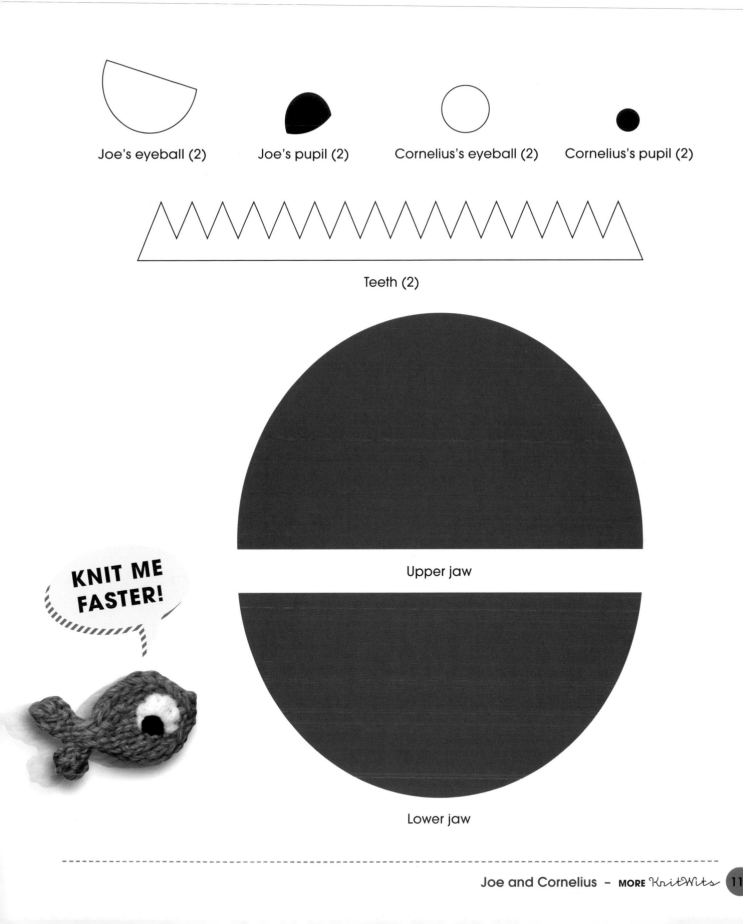

Joe's eyeball (2) Joe's pupil (2) Cornelius's eyeball (2) Cornelius's pupil (2)

Teeth (2)

Upper jaw

Lower jaw

KNIT ME FASTER!

Mr. Maxwell

Mr. Maxwell is a professor of French poetry at the local university. He wears a disguise so that he doesn't alarm his students. Truthfully, he never would have gotten the position if the faculty had any idea he was a monster. He wears the suit and hat to look "normal." The moustache isn't even real. He cuts the hair from his head and then tapes it to his face. Mr. Maxwell felt having a moustache would distract his colleagues from noticing that he only has one eye.

Materials

- 1 skein Cascade 220 in 8021 (MC) beige
- 1 skein Cascade 220 in 8505 (CC1) white
- 1 skein Cascade 220 in 2413 (CC2) rust
- 1 skein Cascade 220 in 2411 (CC3) brown
- 1 set US size 6 (4.00mm) double pointed needles
- Yarn needle
- Embroidery needle
- Craft felt in black, white, blue, medium brown, and dark brown
- Embroidery floss in black, white, blue, medium brown, and dark brown
- Toy stuffing

Gauge:
20 sts and 26 rows over 4 in. in stockinette st

Finished toy size:
8 in. tall.

Glossary of abbreviations

CO	cast on
k	knit
k2tog	knit two together
kfb	knit into front and back of stitch
p	purl
pm	place marker
st[s]	stitch[es]

Body
Knit from the top down
Using MC, CO6, pm, join to knit in the round.
Round 1: Kfb 6 times. 12 sts
Round 2 and all even numbered rounds: Knit.
Round 3: (Kfb, k1) 6 times. 18 sts
Round 5: (Kfb, k2) 6 times. 24 sts
Round 7: (Kfb, k3) 6 times. 30 sts
Round 9: (Kfb, k4) 6 times. 36 sts
Rounds 10–21: Knit.
Switch to CC1.
Rounds 22–34: Knit.
Switch to CC2.
Rounds 35–44: Knit.
Begin dividing for legs
Using CC2, knit the first 18 sts, dividing them between three needles as you go, 6 sts on each needle. Place the last 18 sts on a piece of scrap yarn. Using a fourth needle, CO6 sts as the inside edge of the first leg. Pm, join the knit in the round,

(see figure 1). Stuff the body before beginning knitting.
Rounds 1–6: Knit. 24 sts
Round 7: (K2tog, k2) 6 times. 18 sts
Round 8: Knit.
Round 9: (K2tog, k1) 6 times. 12 sts
Round 10: K2tog 6 times. 6 sts
Break yarn, knot, pull tail into leg. Stuff leg firmly.
Reattach CC2 at front center to begin 2nd leg. Pick up and knit 18 sts from scrap yarn, dividing between 3 needles, 6 sts on each needle. Pick up and knit 6 sts from inside of first leg. Pm, join to knit in the round. Follow the directions as for first leg, pausing to stuff fully before closing up.

Jacket
Back of jacket
Using two double pointed needles and CC3, CO14. Begin knitting straight.
Row 1: Knit.

Row 2: Purl.
Row 3: K1, kfb, k10, kfb, k1. 16 sts
Row 4: Purl.
Row 5: Knit.
Row 6: Purl.
Row 7: K1, kfb, k12, kfb, k1. 18 sts
Row 8: Purl.
Leave sts on needle. front.

Right front
Using two double pointed needles and CC3, CO3.
Row 1: Kfb, k2. 4 sts
Row 2: Purl.
Row 3: Kfb, k2, kfb. 6 sts
Row 4: Purl.
Row 5: Kfb, k5. 7 sts
Row 6: Purl.
Row 7: Kfb, k5, kfb. 9 sts
Row 8: Purl.
Leave sts on needle.

Left front

Using two double pointed needles and CC3, CO2.

Row 1: K1, kfb. 3 sts
Row 2: Purl.
Row 3: Kfb, k1, kfb, 5 sts
Row 4: Purl.
Row 5: K4, kfb. 6 sts
Row 6: Purl.
Row 7: Kfb, k4, kfb. 8 sts
Row 8: Purl.

Break yarn. Connect pieces of jacket as follows. Reconnect yarn at edge of right front. Knit across 9 sts, knit across the 8 sts from left front. Then knit across 18 sts from back. Pm, join to knit in the round. 37 sts, (see figure 2). Knit 8 rounds even. Bind off.

Sleeves (knit 2)

Using two double pointed needles and CC3, CO4. Begin knitting straight.

Row 1: Kfb, k2, kfb. 6 sts
Row 2: Purl.
Row 3: Kfb, k4, kfb. 8 sts
Row 4: Purl.
Row 5: Kfb, k6, kfb. 10 sts
Row 6: Purl.
Row 7: Kfb, k8, kfb. 12 sts
Row 8: Purl.
Divide sts between needles, pm, join to knit in the round.
Round 1: Kfb, k10, kfb. 14 sts
Round 2: Knit.
Rounds 3–4: Knit.
Bind off.

Hands (knit 2)

Using MC, CO6, pm, join to knit in the round.

Round 1: Kfb 6 times. 12 sts
Rounds 2–5: Knit.
Bind off.

Assembly

- - - - - - - - - -

Jacket

Lightly press the jacket and sleeves. Seam the sleeves to jacket, beginning at upper edge of sleeve, working under the arm, and back up other side, (see figure 3). Insert the hands into sleeves. Using CC3, sew along the outside edge of the sleeve, through the hand underneath, (see figure 4).

Stuff the arms inside the jacket.
Cut pieces of felt using template. Center the collar along the top edge of the white section of the body. Sew into place using white thread.
Center the tie in the collar. Sew into place, (see figure 5).
Slip the jacket over the body. Line up the top edge of the jacket with the collar. Place the lapel over the jacket, starting at the center front, stretching around the back and meeting in the front. Sew into place using brown thread, through the jacket and body underneath, (see figure 6).
Center the eye on the front of the face, using a coordinating color of thread. Center the moustache underneath the eye. Tack into place at the top and bottom with brown thread.

Hat

Fold the side of the hat into a circle. Use brown thread to secure, (see figure 7). Place the top of the hat on top of the circle. Use brown thread to secure in place, (see figure 8). Place the top of the hat on the brim and sew into place, (see figure 9). Place the hat on top of the head. Tack into place.

1

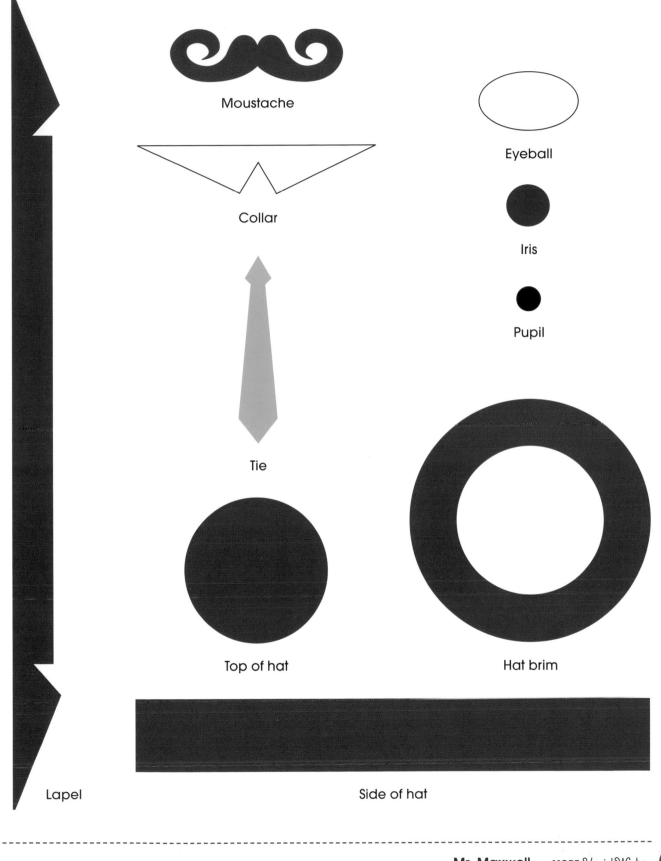

Moustache

Eyeball

Collar

Iris

Pupil

Tie

Top of hat

Hat brim

Lapel

Side of hat

Commode-O-Dragon

"You were in there so long, we'd thought you'd fallen in!" said Meredith's friends as she returned to the table. Then they noticed Meredith was soaking wet. Yes, Meredith had encountered that most terrible of monsters, the Commode-o-Dragon. Cleverly disguised as a toilet, Commode-o-Dragon makes quick and soggy work of her prey. Meredith was very lucky to have escaped with only a dunk.

Materials

- 1 skein Cascade 220 Wool in 8505 (MC)
- 1 skein Cascade 220 Superwash in 878 (CC)
- 1 set US size 6 (4.00mm) double pointed needles
- 1 pair US size 6 (4.00mm) straight needles
- 1 set US size 4 (3.50mm) double pointed needles
- Toy stuffing
- Pieces of wool felt in blue and white
- Embroidery floss in white
- Yarn needle
- Embroidery needle

Gauge:
20 sts and 26 rows over 4 in. in stockinette st

Finished toy size:
10 in. tall.

Glossary of abbreviations

BO	bind off
CO	cast on
k	knit
k2tog	knit two together
kfb	knit into front and back of stitch
p	purl
pm	place marker
ssk	slip, slip, knit slipped stitches together
st[s]	stitch[es]
w&t	wrap and turn

Toilet

Base

Left side

Using size 6 (4.00mm) straight needles, CO4.

Row 1: Kfb, k3. 5 sts

Row 2 and all even numbered rows: Purl.

Row 3: Kfb, k4. 6 sts

Continue to work in stockinette st, increasing one st at the beginning of every other row until you have 15 sts. Place these sts on scrap yarn.

Right side

Row 1: K3, kfb. 5 sts

Row 2 and all even numbered rows: Purl.

Row 3: K4, kfb. 6 sts

Continue to work in stockinette st, increasing one st at the end of every other row until you have 15 sts. CO10 sts.

Break yarn. Place the 15 sts from scrap yarn on the same needle, (see figure 1). Reattach yarn at left side to begin purling.

Row 1: Purl. 40 sts

Rows 2–11: Complete in stockinette st.

Row 12: BO15, k10, BO15. 10 sts

Break yarn. Reattach at left edge of remaining sts to begin purling.

Row 13: Purl.

Row 14: Kfb, k8, kfb. 12 sts

Rows 15–17: Work in stockinette st.

Row 18: Kfb, k10, kfb. 14 sts

Rows 19–21: Work in stockinette st.

Row 22: Kfb, 12, kfb. 16 sts

Rows 23–25: Work in stockinette st.

Row 26: Kfb, 14, kfb. 18 sts

Rows 27–36: Work in stockinette st

Row 37: Ssk, k14, k2tog. 16 sts

Rows 38–40: Work in stockinette st

Row 41: Ssk, k12, k2tog. 14 sts

Rows 42–44: Work in stockinette st

Row 45: Ssk, k10, k2tog. 12 sts

Rows 46–48: Work in stockinette st

Row 49: Ssk, k8, k2tog. 10 sts

Work 10 more rows in stockinette st. Bind off, leaving a 12in. tail for seaming.

Bowl

Using MC and US size 6 (4.00mm) double pointed needles, CO6, pm, join to knit in the round.

Round 1: Kfb 6 times. 12 sts

Round 2 and all even numbered rounds: Knit.

Round 3: (Kfb, k1) 6 times. 18 sts

Round 5: (Kfb, k2) 6 times. 24 sts

Round 7: (Kfb, k3) 6 times. 30 sts

Round 9: (Kfb, k4) 6 times. 36 sts

Round 11: (Kfb, k5) 6 times. 42 sts

Round 13: (Kfb, k6) 6 times. 48 sts

Round 15: (Kfb, k7) 6 times. 54 sts

Round 17: (Kfb, k8) 6 times. 60 sts

Knit 5 rounds evenly. Bind off.

Top of bowl

Using MC and US size 6 (4.00mm) straight needles, CO11.

Row 1: K1, kfb, k7, kfb, k1. 13 sts

Row 2 and all even numbered rows: Purl.

Row 3: K1, kfb, k9, kfb, k1. 15 sts

Row 5: K1, kfb, k11, kfb, k1. 17 sts

Row 7: K1, kfb, k13, kfb, k1. 19 sts

Row 9: K1, kfb, k15, kfb, k1. 21 sts

Rows 10–22: Complete in stockinette st.

Row 23: K1, k2tog, k15, ssk, k1. 19 sts

Row 25: K1, k2tog, k13, ssk, k1. 17 sts
Row 27: K1, k2tog, k11, ssk, k1. 15 sts
Row 29: K1, k2tog, k9, ssk, k1. 13 sts
Row 31: K1, k2tog, k7, ssk, k1. 11 sts
Bind off purlwise. Leave a 24 in. tail
for seaming.

Toilet seat
Using MC and US size 6 (4.00mm)
straight needles, CO11.
Row 1: K1, kfb, k7, kfb, k1. 13 sts
Row 2 and all even rows: Purl.
Row 3: K1, kfb, k9, kfb, k1. 15 sts
Row 5: K1, kfb, k11, kfb, k1. 17 sts
Row 7: K1, kfb, k13, kfb, k1. 19 sts
Row 9: K1, kfb, k6, BO3, k6, kfb, k1. 18 sts
Row 10: Purl 9 sts. Place remaining 9
sts on a stitch holder or double pointed
needle. Turn to begin left side of seat.
Row 11: K1, k2tog, k4, kfb, k1. 9 sts
Row 12–22: Complete in stockinette st.
Row 23: K1, kfb, k4, ssk, k1.
Row 24: Purl.
Break yarn. Put 9 sts on a stitch holder
or double pointed needle. Weave in tail.
Reattach yarn to knit sts on other holder,
beginning with a purl row.
Row 10: Purl.
Row 11: K1, kfb, k4, ssk, k1. 9 sts
Rows 12–22: Complete in stockinette st.
Row 23: K1, k2tog, k4, kfb, k1.
Row 24: Purl.
Row 25: K1, k2tog, k4, kfb, k1, CO3.
12 sts
Place sts from left side next to right side
and begin knitting across as follows: K1,
kfb, k4, ssk, k1. 21 sts
Row 26 and all even rows: Purl.
Row 27: K1, k2tog, k15, ssk, k1. 19 sts
Row 29: K1, k2tog, k13, ssk, k1. 17 sts
Row 31: K1, k2tog, k11, ssk, k1. 15 sts
Row 33: K1, k2tog, k9, ssk, k1. 13 sts
Row 35: K1, k2tog, k7, ssk, k1. 11 sts
Bind off purlwise, leaving a 15 in. tail
for seaming.

Lid
Using US size 6 (4.00mm) double
pointed needles and MC, CO22, pm,
join to knit in the round.

Round 1: (K1, kfb, k7, kfb, k1) twice.
26 sts
Round 2 and all even rows: Knit.
Round 3: (K1, kfb, k9, kfb, k1) twice.
30 sts
Round 5: (K1, kfb, k11, kfb, k1) twice.
34 sts
Round 7: (K1, kfb, k13, kfb, k1) twice.
38 sts
Round 9: (K1, kfb, k15, kfb, k1) twice.
42 sts
Rounds 10–22: Knit.
Round 23: (K1, k2tog, k15, ssk, k1)
twice. 38 sts
Round 25: (K1, k2tog, k13, ssk, k1)
twice. 34 sts
Round 27: (K1, k2tog, k11, ssk, k1)
twice. 30 sts
Round 29: (K1, k2tog, k9, ssk, k1) twice.
26 sts
Round 31: (K1, k2tog, k7, ssk, k1) twice.
22 sts
Bind off. Sew both openings closed.
Do not stuff.

Tank
Using US size 6 (4.00mm) double
pointed needles and MC, CO18.
The first section is knit straight. Begin
with a knit row.
Rows 1–12: Work in stockinette st.
Row 13: K18, CO38. 56 sts
Pm, join to knit in the round.
Knit 20 rounds even.
Round 34: K18, BO38. 18 sts
Return to knitting straight. Work 12 rows
in stockinette st. Bind off.

Legs (knit 2)
Using US size 4 (3.5mm) double pointed
needles and CC, CO12, pm, join to knit
in the round.
Rounds 1–5: Knit.
Round 6: K1, kfb, k8, kfb, k1. 14 sts
Round 7: Knit.
Round 8: K2, kfb, k8, kfb, k2. 16 sts
Round 9: Knit.
Round 10: K3, kfb, k8, kfb, k3. 18 st
Rounds 11–13: Knit.
Round 14: K3, k2tog, k8, ssk, k3. 16 sts

Round 15: K2, k2tog, k8, ssk, k2. 14 sts
Round 16: K1, k2tog, k8, ssk, k1. 12 sts
Rounds 17–18: Knit.
Begin short row shaping for knee.
Round 19: K11, w&t.
Round 20: P10, w&t.
Round 21: K9, w&t.
Round 22: P8, w&t.
Round 23: K7, w&t.
Round 24: P6, w&t.
Round 25: K7, w&t.
Round 26: P8, w&t.
Round 27: K9, w&t.
Round 28: P10, w&t.
End short row shaping. Return to knitting
in the round.
Round 29: Knit.
Round 30: K1, kfb, k8, kfb, k1. 14 sts
Round 31: Knit.
Round 32: K2, kfb, k8, kfb, k2. 16 sts
Round 33: Knit.
Round 34: K3, kfb, k8, kfb, k3. 18 sts
Round 35: Knit, turn.
Begin knitting straight to shape opening:
Row 36: P2tog, p14, p2tog. 16 sts
Row 37 and all remaining odd rows: Knit.
Row 38: P2tog, p12, p2tog. 14 sts
Row 40: P2tog, p10, p2tog. 12 sts
Row 42: P2tog, p8, p2tog. 10 sts
Row 44: P2tog, p6, p2tog. 8 sts
Row 46: P2tog, p4, p2tog. 6 sts
Bind off.

Feet (knit 2)
Using US size 4 (3.5mm) double pointed
needles and CC, CO6, pm, join to knit in
the round.
Round 1: Kfb 6 times. 12 sts
Round 2: (K1, kfb, k2, kfb, k1) twice.
16 sts
Rounds 3–5: Knit.
Round 6: K1, ssk, k10, k2tog, k1. 14 sts
Rounds 7–8: Knit.
Round 9: K1, kfb, k10, kfb, k1. 16 sts
Round 10: K1, kfb, k12, kfb, k1. 18 sts
Round 11: K1, kfb, k14, kfb, k1. 20 sts
Round 12: Knit.
Pause and stuff foot lightly.
Round 13: K8, k2tog, ssk, k8. 18 sts
Round 14: K7, k2tog, ssk, k7. 16 sts

Round 15: K6, k2tog, ssk, k6. 14 sts
Round 16: K1, ssk, k4, k2tog, ssk, k4, k2tog, k1. 10 sts
Bind off. Seam end of foot closed with tail.

Big toe (knit 2)
Using US size 4 (3.5mm) double pointed needles and CC, CO4.

Knit 3 rounds of i-cord. Break yarn, pull tail through sts.

Small toes (knit 8)
Using size 4 double pointed needles and CC, CO3.
Knit 2 rounds of i-cord. Break yarn, pull tail through sts.

Assembly

Base
Lightly press piece. Flattening it will help with seaming. Take the two small cast on edges and seam together. Wrap the center long flat piece around and underneath to create sort of an oblong cup. Pin into place and seam together, (see figure 2). Stuff base.

Bowl
Lightly press the top of the bowl. Center over bowl and seam into place, pausing to stuff firmly when ¾ done. Cut a blue oval from the felt using the template. Center on top of the bowl and sew into place, (see figure 3). Lightly press the toilet seat.

Place over bowl, and seam around the outside edge only, (see figure 4).
Place the bowl on base. Pin into place if needed. Seam together, (see figure 5).

Tank
Open the tank like a box, and fold one side over. Seam into place. Stuff the tank squeezing and prodding it into a box shape. Fold top flap down, and sew into place. Center the tank on top of the back of the base. Seam into place along the back, and along the edge of the seat, (see figure 6).

Lid
Place lid on top of bowl. Sew to back edge of tank, (see figure 7).

Cut felt pieces using template. All pieces are cut from two thicknesses of felt to create stiffness. Pair the pieces together, and use white thread to whipstitch the edges together. Center small teeth on front of top lid. Sew into place. Sew large teeth on the sides of the seat, (see figure 8). Sew the handle onto the front of the tank.

Legs
Stuff the legs. Sew the toes to the tops of the feet, starting with the big toes, (see figure 9). Sew the feet to the smaller edge of the legs. Use flesh colored thread to sew the legs onto inside of the toilet bowl, (see figure 10).

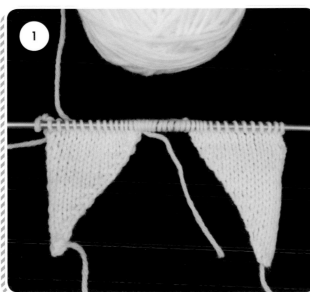

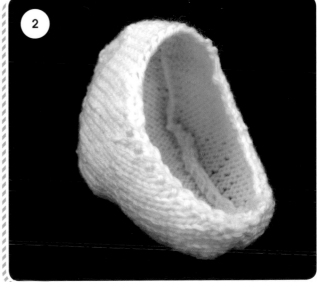

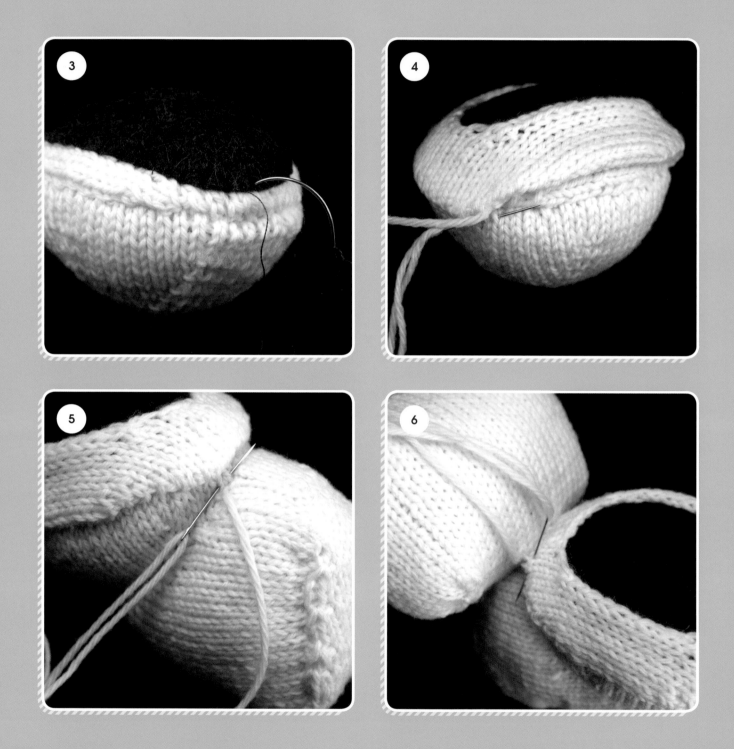

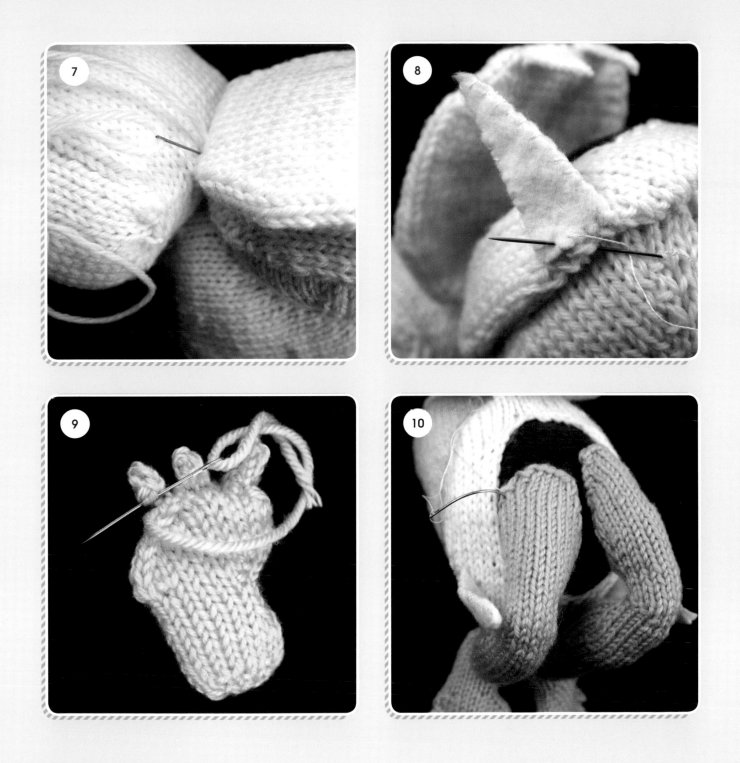

Large teeth (4)

Small teeth (4)

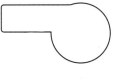

Handle (2)

Difficulty Key and Acknowledgments

= Beginner   = Intermediate   = Seasoned

Cascade is a manufacturer and international distributor of fine yarns, their products are available worldwide. I thank them for supplying all the yarns used in this book.

Katie Boyette

In the late 1980s, Bob and Jean Dunbabin founded Cascade Yarns in Seattle, Washington with the goal to provide affordable, high-quality yarns. The search for a soft, long-stapled wool brought Bob Dunbabin to Peru, where he found plentiful, light-colored, high lofting wool from sheep (a hybrid of the native Corriedale and Merino) that were raised by Peruvian natives in the Sierra Mountains above 12,000 feet. Largely by word-of-mouth, Cascade 220 became renowned as the affordable high-quality knitting yarn with great yardage that is available in more than 350 Solids, Heathers, Quatros, Tweeds, and Hand Paints.